Darling, Yours Always

THE WORLD WAR II LETTERS OF
PEGGY AND GEORGE STEINER
1941-1943

VOLUME I

Compiled, Edited and Annotated by

Art Mendoza-Ballesteros

ISBN: 978-1-7355659-1-0

Letters and photographs from the collection of Georgia Steiner

Cover design by David James

Printed in the United States of America

This book is dedicated to the brave and diligent supporters behind the "front lines," who kept the troops supplied and the home fires burning.

—Georgia

TABLE OF CONTENTS

STEINER/GILLETTE FAMILY TREE

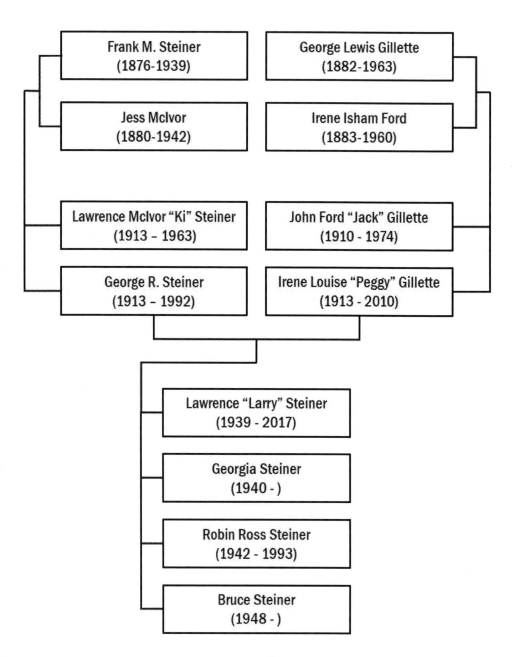

Frank M. Steiner
(1876-1939)

George Lewis Gillette
(1882-1963)

Jess McIvor
(1880-1942)

Irene Isham Ford
(1883-1960)

Lawrence McIvor "Ki" Steiner
(1913 – 1963)

John Ford "Jack" Gillette
(1910 - 1974)

George R. Steiner
(1913 – 1992)

Irene Louise "Peggy" Gillette
(1913 - 2010)

Lawrence "Larry" Steiner
(1939 - 2017)

Georgia Steiner
(1940 -)

Robin Ross Steiner
(1942 - 1993)

Bruce Steiner
(1948 -)

INTRODUCTION

It is tempting to see World War II only as the massive, worldwide conflict that it was, but in that abstraction what it meant to be one of the millions living during that time is lost. Personal accounts of real people and their daily struggles and triumphs during major historical events are critical because without these observations, era-defining moments can become solely objects of study, losing their human connection. This collection of letters bears witness to a unique set of challenges—those of Irene "Peggy" Gillette, an American woman living in the United States, and those of her husband George R. Steiner, a WWII officer managing the minutia of war support logistics supplying the front.

The exact details of George's military service are unknown, as his personnel file is missing and believed to be among the many that burned in the 1973 National Archives fire. Aside from the information that George graduated from Yale as a member of the Reserve Officer Training Corps shortly before his wedding, what is known about his service comes from pieces of information assembled from different organizations and an eight-page biography Peggy wrote for her grandchildren. In it she writes that George was called up shortly after their first son's birth in February 1939 and stationed at an airbase in Rome, New York, but was unable to become a pilot because he was nearsighted. Consequently, George was assigned to the Army Air Corps G-4, the unit responsible for readying, planning, and monitoring Army Air Corps units throughout the war. G-4 divisions are also responsible for providing equipment, supplies and services, as well as coordinating transportation and maintenance but it is difficult to confirm with which sub-division George was associated.

This letter collection begins in 1941, before the United States officially enters the war but with George already living apart from his wife and two young children, Larry and Georgia. It stops in mid-1943 when George is sent overseas. During this time, Peggy and George wrote to each other sometimes twice a week, and these letters make up this volume.

This collection speaks not only of a physical time in the past, but of values that are disappearing in a world which seems to encourage convenience and instant gratification. Letters were not mere retellings of daily activities. They were the only way many could imagine the experiences their loved ones were having a world away. In this collection of stateside letters, Peggy and George have the luxury of occasional visits and phone calls. Unknown to the two writers, the letters will soon be their only way to connect once George is sent overseas.

Darling, Yours Always captivates because both writers communicate honestly and openly with each other. The letters range from humorous anecdotes, history lessons, and gentle teasing to profound expressions of love, loneliness, and loss. For Peggy and George, each written word was an intimate expression of a memory, a shared joke, or a confession of a struggle. Each letter is a gesture—an invitation to immerse oneself in the reality of another.

EDITOR'S NOTE

Many personal accounts during WWII are one-sided or centered around the observations of a sole author. This often requires extensive narration or elaborate endnotes by an editor to fill in gaps so the reader has context to follow the story. I have included every letter that was made available to me in this collection so that Peggy and George's voices flow naturally without any additional narrative techniques by an outsider, enabling the reader to better focus on Peggy and George's story.

Letters that appear in this collection are almost entirely as they appear in their original form. Grammatical errors that might affect the reader's understanding have been corrected. Examples of this include missing periods to end sentences and apostrophes incorrectly placed or omitted that would otherwise change the meaning. Any names that may have been spelled in multiple ways have been kept as they appear in the originals, despite the inconsistency. Any words that I have added to improve clarity are noted in brackets. In order to preserve the style of the physical letters as much as possible, various markings and symbols, as well as grammar errors that do not impede the reader's comprehension, have been left as they appear in the originals.

Dates were the greatest challenge with assembling this collection. The majority of letters are dated only by abbreviated day, for example, "Wed." or "Saturday pm." There are also occasions where the letters are dated *after* their postmark date. I am not the first person to work with this collection, so it is possible that envelopes were mixed up or lost. It is also possible that the United States Postal Service occasionally made mistakes, as evidenced by my favorite envelope, postmarked, "November 31, 1942." Sunday postmarks appear as well, suggesting that stamping the wrong date was not so unusual. Also, Peggy and George were busy people who lost track of the date or day when they wrote and thus, they guessed. I have left their indications of day or date on their letters and in the brackets above I have noted postmarks and the nearest date that matches the day they wrote. For letters without envelopes, I have guessed and written "probably" or "possibly" so that the reader knows the letter placement is an estimate based on events described in the letter.

I have included brief footnotes for the interested reader but they are intended as supplements to the letters. All research is cited in the footnotes and the citations utilize an abbreviation key that can be found in the Abbreviations section. Information in the footnotes that is not cited (usually regarding people or places) is information provided to me by Georgia, additional family documents, or the letters themselves. Any names in the letters that do not have a corresponding footnote are people I could not identify and Georgia did not remember.

Any mistakes in identifying people and places are mine and I apologize for any inconsistencies I may have overlooked.

1941

[To Peggy]
[Handwritten on 8/11/41, postmarked on 8/12/41 at 11 AM]
[From Edgewood Arsenal, MD[1] to Greenwich, CT]

Peggy dear,

Just a short note before going to bed to tell you how much I enjoyed the weekend. It was a real thrill to see you and the children. I am happy to see how well you looked. Larry and Georgia are just perfect. I keep thinking of that darling little girl with a big smile when I went in to kiss her good bye. Larry was so much fun to play

---

[1] Edgewood Arsenal was created in 1917 to "research, design, develop, engineer, produce, and test every chemical and biological defense piece of equipment, smoke/obscuration system, medical-related tool, flame and incendiary weapon, riot control device, retaliatory chemical weapon and demilitarization device" used by the U.S. Armed Forces in WWI and on (ROM – see ABBREVIATIONS). Unlike other chemical warfare locations which were shut down after WWI ended, Edgewood remained operational. During WWII, Edgewood saw an increase in the production of defensive equipment and retaliatory weapons as well as an expansion of the Chemical School program, the Armed Forces' center for chemical weapons research and training. In 1993, a secret government program to test chemical agents on American troops was declassified revealing a decades-long practice of using American servicemen as experimental subjects (DIC). It was not until 2008 that a Canadian researcher discovered that the soldiers forced to participate in the experiments were usually soldiers of African-American, Japanese, or Puerto Rican descent (SMI2).

Toxic materials were not only tested at Edgewood but stored and disposed of as well. In 1971, the Edgewood Arsenal merged with the nearby Aberdeen Proving Ground, long considered one of the country's most polluted military bases and currently the nation's third most expensive cleanup (SAB]

George attended the "Unit Gas Officers' Course (Aviation)" of the Chemical Warfare School at the Edgewood Arsenal from July 21-August 16, 1941. A first lieutenant at the time, George graduated on August 16 along with 57 other students (CWS).

with, and still a nicely behaved little fellow.

I was sorry to have to leave you so soon dear, and am anxious looking forward to spending every minute of that leave with you. Thank you for the nice party, after this life here it was doubly appreciated. It was mighty nice of you to come in town with me last night.

After I had turned my examination in this morning the instructor called me aside, telling me that I had made a rather formidable impression on the officers in the school to the extent they would like to have me remain here as an instructor having picked me out of several hundred men who have gone through here in the last few months. It depends on two things: first whether I want the job, then whether the commanding officer of the air corps unit to which I have been assigned wishes to release me for this duty with Chemical Warfare. I am still thinking it over, but being pleased with the compliment I thought I would tell you. That is what Frank said last night that I would quite probably be detailed as an instructor. The advantage would be that we would be quite certain of not being shifted around. But I am still interested in Salt Lake.

All my love, dear, and I am looking forward to Saturday.

Yours,

George

[To Peggy]
[Handwritten[2] on 11/11/41, postmarked on 11/11/41[3]]
[From Southern Pines, NC[4] to Greenwich, CT]

Peggy dear,

This has been a good change from the monotony of camp life with a chance thrown in to get well cleaned up and wash out some clothes. After I talked to you last night I had wash all over the place: six drawers, six pair soxs, 1pr. woolen pajamas, five handkerchiefs, 2 bath towels, and 2 wash clothes.

It sounded as if you had a mean cold last night. Please don't go running into the city while you have a cold. It was just about this time of year that we got pneumonia, so please take good care of yourself. I wonder if the dry air when you start using the furnace

---

[2] A photo of this stationery is included in the Memories section.

[3] Veteran's Day 1941.

[4] Originally called the Knollwood Airport, the U.S. Army Air Corps leased the airfield from 1942-1945, temporarily renaming it the Knollwood Army Auxiliary Airfield. The airfield was initially used as a communications training base. In 1943, the airfield played an important role in the Knollwood Maneuver, the famous experimental maneuver that convinced U.S. generals of the viability of an attack led by a large-scale airborne formation. After the war, the airfield was renamed the Pinehurst-Southern Pines Airport. It is now called the Moore County Airport (DAV).

doesn't make it easier to get a cold. Write soon and let me know how you are.

I played golf today. Tonight I am going to have dinner here then let the garage man drive me back down to camp. I have left the car at a garage, Pages in Southern Pines, right across from the railroad station. Before I go out to camp I will drive over to Pinehurst to pick up the car keys which the Peakes left at the Holly Inn. I am sorry that I missed them.

Tonight I am going to wear my brown suit to dinner, it is so good to get out of a uniform. And it felt mighty nice last night to sleep between the sheets, even though I could not wear my one and only pair of woolen pajamas as they were wet.

Crawling between the sheets without any pajamas didn't seem just proper without you there. Then when I was taking a bath I remembered how much fun you and I had had one night. I hope that happens again some time.

Probably because I had been thinking about you before I went to sleep, I dreamt that you were lying here with me. Perhaps I had not better write all that I dreamt of, but it was all about you dear. Next time you are in my arms it will be much nicer than dreaming though, because imagine my surprise when I woke up to find my arms around a pillow.

Which all reminds me of the mention you made of a double bed last night. I wish we had one in the house, because when we sleep together I always seem to be hanging on to the sheets to keep from rolling out of bed. Maybe it is because you sleep cross wise, but I think it is principally, because a single bed is only built for one person to use. If you can still get it and have a place to use it I would like to have a double bed.

Now how did I ever get off on such matters. Guess I must still be in love. Don't you think that I ought to know better than to write like this at my age.

What I really want to do when this is over here is for you and I to have a party for ourselves in New York. I want you all dressed up in an evening gown, the one we got in Paris, with flowers from me, and I will dress too. I will be so proud of my girl. We will have dinner at the Cremailles[5], see a play, then go dinner dancing. Is that a date?

_____

[5] This name is possibly misspelled by the editor.

I wish I had been with you last night to look at our wedding movies. It is a lot more difficult to get in to call you now so don't worry if I do not get a chance to phone for a while again. As soon as I find out definitely what my plans will be for leaving here I will let you know. I hope that I can get up there for a day or you can get down here before this is all over, three weeks is a long time.

Show Larry what a long, long letter Daddy wrote, all because he loves Mama and his little family so much. Tell me what Georgia is doing now. Can she say anything yet.

My best to Irene.

All my love.
George

[To Peggy]
[Handwritten on 11/27/41, postmarked on 11/21/41[6] at 6 PM]
[From Southern Pines, NC to Greenwich, CT]

Darling:

This is the first time I have spent a Thanksgiving like this, no turkey, no cranberry sauce, just army routine. It is hard to realize that it is Thanksgiving. But there are a lot of things to be thankful for at that. We are both a lot better off than we were three years ago at this time. All the ones that are dear to us are healthy and well provided for. And above all I have the finest girl in the world, with the swellest little boy and cutest little girl that ever was. I do love you so very much dear. It was so nice to talk to you last night, your voice sounded so pleased when you answered the phone. It pleased me more than a little to hear you say you loved me, even though I know it so well. It is getting to be an awful long time since I saw you.

I don't know just when we will be able to leave here yet, but

---

[6] This letter was possibly placed in the wrong envelope as Thanksgiving was on Thursday, November 27, 1941.

the maneuvers will surely be over by the end of next week. It may be a few days after the end of this month before we can get everything cleared up here so we can leave. I am quite sure that I cannot get home by a week from Saturday, but will certainly try as I would like to see George and Irene[7]. I will call you up just as soon as I find out when I can leave and hope we can meet in Washington. You might look up the train schedule as I cannot get ahold of one here. If I can leave here in the morning and meet you up there in the afternoon we could stay there or in Baltimore for the night and drive home the next day.

I received the pajamas and gloves which were very welcome. Thank you for getting all of the Christmas presents. I don't know just what I can get for my best girl, but it is going to have to be something pretty nice. I will take care of the few presents left to get.

I am looking forward to a real Christmas day with you, Larry and Georgia. And I am not forgetting about our date for a party in

---

[7] Peggy's parents, George Gillette and Irene Isham Ford Gillette.

New York. I think we will be just about due to do right by a bottle of Champagne.

The time seems to go so slowly when I keep thinking about getting home to you dear. But there have been some more interesting events going on here during the last week. General Arnold[8] stopped here the other day. He is a fine looking man and the men with him give you confidence that we have some real leadership in the air force. There are blackouts every night, bombing attacks, and parachute troops dropped around us.

I will write soon again dear and am anxious to get your letter tomorrow.

With so much love,
George

---

[8] Most likely General Henry "Hap" Arnold, widely known as the father of the modern American Air Force. He was placed in command of the Army Air Corps in 1938 and is credited with turning it into the enormously successful organization it became during WWII (COF).

1942

[To Peggy]
[Probably written in early May 1942[9]]
[Probably from Key West, FL[10] to unknown]

Most important first of all I love you very much and miss you too much. I was sorry to hear of your trouble, but glad it was no mor[e] serious. Do be careful of yourself dear, remember, you are my favorite wife, and that I am just living now so that I may be with you again. I look forward to that time when we can be together permanently again. We will have everything as we have always planned it, I promise you my dear.

Enough of that, but there is lots more going on inside me all day as my dear Peggy is often in my thoughts during the day.

You probably want to know about this place. It is quite out of the ordinary as airports go. There are the usual two runways NE to SW and one N to S with the ocean bending around to the south side

---

[9] Most likely written shortly after George arrived at the Naval Air Station in Key West, Florida (STE 1991, 1).

[10] George was stationed in Key West, in command of a group of 22 men who were tasked with providing aviation gasoline to military planes using the airfields at Meacham Field (STE 1991, 1).

with nothing in sight but the horizon. Between the field and the ocean is an old red brick fort built just before the Civil War.[11] It has a center building, just like the high "keeps" of the old castles, surrounded by lower outerwalls. Part of it is in ruins with bushes and even trees growing up out of the crumbled walls. The center "keep" was more solidly built in its outer walls at least so the coast artillery have a small observation post on top and the infantry furnish us machine guns and extra guards. The old gun galleries which are in better condition than most of the place we use for a kitchen and mess hall. Our tents where we sleep are just outside the main gate to the north. It is arranged something like this:

---

[11] The U.S. first occupied Key West in 1822, establishing what later became known as the Key West Barracks in 1831 (ROB, 209). George is most likely referencing the East Martello Tower, built at the beginning of the Civil War to help fortify Key West (specifically the nearby West Martello Tower and Fort Taylor) (ROB, 184-185, 209). The East Martello Tower, now a museum, abuts the Key West International Airport, the modern-day incarnation of Meacham Field.

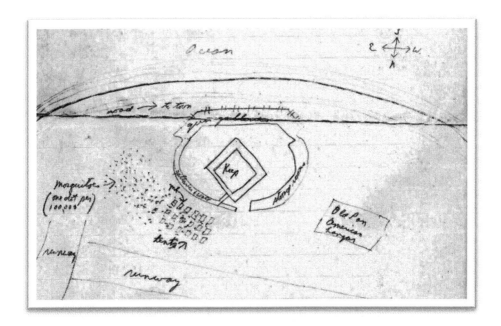

It is quite a picturesque old place. I am going to find out all about [it] and you will have to listen even if you go to sleep in my arms while I am telling you about it. You can be sure that I have climbed all over the place by now. Key West I find was held by the Union forces all through the Civil War.[12] Just a secret to you, I get quite a thrill out of being C.O. of a real old time fort, and much

---

[12] Despite Florida seceding and joining the Confederate States of America, the naval base at Key West remained in Union hands. The Confederacy was dependent on Europe for manufactured material during the Civil War, thus it was a Union priority to create a blockade along the entire Gulf of Mexico. Union control of Florida and the Keys sealed off the eastern side of the Gulf to any ships from Europe attempting to drop off aid to the South. (THO, 17).

prefer it to a brand new air base.

In my maps you will note the old Pan American hangar. All that is left of it is a concrete floor, but it interested [me] as I found that it was the first home of the Pan American Airlines whose first run was from Key West to Havana.[13] They have not used the field for a number of years.

Gen. Drum[14] and other high rankers come in here often. There is a lot to be done here as the former officer did not manage to get much done and living conditions are a bit tough. The only water has to be hauled out by tank trailer about 7 miles and it is quite limited.[15] The men have practically no place to wash and the sanitary facilities are better not mentioned. However we will do a job on it.

---

[13] George is correct. Pan Am began operations in 1927 as an air mail and passenger service between Key West, Florida and Havana, Cuba.

[14] A reference to Lieutenant General Hugh Aloysius Drum who led the Eastern Defense Command, responsible for the United States' defense of the Atlantic seaboard during WWII. Drum was sent to review the Meacham Field Operation and according to George, "was pleased with what he saw" (STE 1991, 2).

[15] Water was brought in from the Key West barracks (STE 1991, 1).

[To George]
[Probably written on 5/5/42[16]]
[Locations unknown]

Dearest George,

I've been on the phone a couple of hours trying to make arrangements for shipping Steppy[17] to Cecil[8]. I'll be so glad when it's over and he has arrived safely. It makes me feel as if I'm deserting my adult child. He was so glad to see me when I got back and stuck his nose in all my pockets. I know Cece will give him a good home though. I think I'll give her his bridle and blanket. What do you think of that saddle. It's pretty well gone, but I don't want to send it if you think Ki[19] would mind.

It's a rather cold morning. Mother has the children outdoors, and the yard looks fine. Tony cut the grass by hand (I got a new hand mower for $15.50) and had time left over to plant me a vegetable garden yesterday. What do you

---

[16] Jessie, George's mother, died on Monday, April 27 and May 5 is the following Tuesday.

[17] Stepson, Peggy's horse.

[18] Cecil (Cece) was Peggy's close friend and roommate from Mount Holyoke.

[19] George's twin brother, officially Lawrence McIvor Steiner, informally known as "Ki."

suppose that Flancher did last year.

I spent a couple of days after you left at 1941 Knox[20] helping Nell pack up the trinkets. She had everything pretty well put away and let me tell you she's the one for you to thank. She refused to even take as much as a bed jacket of Jessies[21] and aside from going through letters etc. Gertrude never did a thing to help her close the house. There were no words about it at all, but I could see Nell was disappointed in Gertrude also. She told me she insisted on Gertrude sending a couple of dresses to each of Teedie[22] and Aunt Helen although G. felt Jess wanted her to take all her clothes. Anyhow, I can assure you everything went smoothly. Nell's making a complete inventory with values attached so that you and Ki can divide things between you when the time comes.

Gertrude asked me to tell you and Ki that she took a set of dishes which matched some she had. I'm not sure which they were, but it's a small matter. I do wish Teedie could

---

[20] The Steiner property where George and Ki grew up in Minneapolis, MN.

[21] George's mother, Jess McIvor Steiner.

[22] The affectionate nickname for Ki's wife, Harriet.

have Jessie's watch though.

I sent both Gertrude and Nell flowers when I left with notes of thanks. When all's done you'll find Nell and Marg are the truly great friends your Mother had.

Mary Olsen[23] came to me the last day and asked me to write you to give her a $5.00 monthly raise. It is really not all in order to my mind. She is getting $75.00 a month out of which to date she's paid room and board. Now she has less work and no room to pay. Mary's nobody's fool and she realizes this is a good time to make a touch. Give Miss Finn[24] any instructions you have on [the] subject.

The children both look grand. Larry has us laughing most of the time. Mom brought him a toy train which is his constant companion. He's made innumerable trips to "Key West for Daddy." How I wish you could see this beautiful spring. If we could only settle down here quietly and never be bothered. This is such an ideal spot to live.

Mother and I went to Marjorie's for dinner last night. Pete's away. Today we're going to lunch at the Woman's

---

[23] The housekeeper who cared for Ki and George when they were growing up.

[24] George's secretary.

Exchange with Jean and Mrs. Beane.

Oh dear, the mailman beat me. Now I can't get this off before noon. We get our gas rationing cards today.

I'm feeling pretty good now, but my clothes are getting tight and how I hate that. If this next 8 months ever goes by I'll be surprised. It's bad enough to miss you and worry about you the way I do without carrying extra care physically too. Do take the very best care of yourself, possible at all times.

Yours always,
Peggy

X   X   X   x

Larry Georgia Me Doxie[25]

---

[25] Doxie was gifted to Peggy as a puppy in 1934 after an accident that left Peggy in a body cast her entire junior year of college.

[To George]
[Handwritten, possibly on 5/8/42[26]]
[Locations unknown[27]]

P.P.S. Just to let you know how badly I need a letter I just reread for the 40-11th time the one you gave me in Minneapolis. Now how about that.

Darling,

I was so glad to see Larry's postal today. I was beginning to worry about you. He's been carrying the card around showing everyone "Daddy's new house." We'll hope for a letter soon.

Well Steppy left yesterday and a large part of my heart went with him. I hope I never love another animal quite so much again. I had a van take him to Portchester freight yards and he behaved like a lamb. He walked out and up the ramp and right into the car. He nuzzled my hands while

---

[26] Steppy has just been sent off to Cecil so this letter is most likely following up on the previous one.

[27] It can be assumed George was already in Key West, Florida, based on his previous letter and the drawing of the base.

they boxed up a stall in the freight car and I fed him
carrots. He looked like a scared baby. The engineer was
ready as soon as the last nail was driven so I patted him on
the nose and climbed out. He just looked at me as if he knew
I was deserting him. I could see him through the crack they
left for air as the engine hitched on and as they jerked him
out of the yard I burst into tears in front of the whole freight
yard crew and all of the van men. Disgusting to say the
least. I'm O.K. now and was then as soon as I could talk
myself into being lucky to have had him six years and now
be able to send him to such a good home. He should reach
Danville Saturday night or Sun. a.m. I've asked Cecil to
wire me when he gets there.

Mother and I are really stuck here. They only gave me
an A card (3 gallons a week).[28] We used up one today

---

[28] On May 15, 1942, the U.S. Office of Price Administration (OPA) began rationing gasoline in 17 eastern states. An "A" card was issued to the general public and contained seven squares, each representing a unit of gasoline. How much gasoline a unit constituted was something that fluctuated based on supply. The "B1," "B2," and "B3" cards were issued to doctors, war workers, and anyone else whose work required a mileage greater than the "A" cards (NYT 04/23/1942, 16). The U.S. began gasoline rationing as a way to save as much rubber as possible for the war effort. Traditional imports of rubber to the U.S. were controlled by the Japanese (NYT 01/02/1942, 47) and in an effort to keep Americans from wearing through their tires, the government made it more difficult to drive cars (NYT 01/04/1942, 1). In her biography, Peggy claims that, "we were about 8 miles from town," thus gas rationing made their daily lives more challenging.

going to Round Hill for bridge game and tea party so now there are two left until a week from today. It's really awful.

I managed to get a B2[29] rating for your car due to your 5 mile commute from Manchester to [the] Air Base each day. It's a bit far fetched, but O.K. I guess. It would be better if I'd gotten 2 A cards cause then I could use yours too. As it is I had to swear the Oldsmobile would not be used until you took it back to Manch. for that purpose. I'm enclosing your card to sign. I wish you would return it though, cause in case of emergency I'm sure Mr. Wamback would help me out.

The children are fine. Robbie[30] came up yesterday. He left for camp today. I wasn't here when he came which was a great disappointment to me. Anna[31] said Georgia was thrilled to death over him and evidently the uniform mixed her up. She kissed and hugged him and picked grass for him. Then at six o'clock this morning she woke us all up calling "Daddy."

---

[29] The B2 card provided for 15 units of gasoline (NYT 04/23/1942, 16).

[30] Frederick Robinson "Robbie" Peake (b. 08/10/1913, d. 11/01/1998) was one of George's closest friends and also a Yale graduate. Georgia believes that her brother Robin was named after him.

[31] Anna was a young woman who worked for the family as a housekeeper and cook.

Mother is doing my mending here for me while I write. Now she's putting a patch in the coat of your yellow pajamas. How I wish you were here and in them instead! Such ideas I have.

I do hope the heat has let up a little—also the mosquitoes. Be sure and write me whenever you can. I'll be home day and night now with no gasoline and your letters will be even more necessary to keep body and soul together if that's possible.

I washed both cars this morning and with Mother's help—cleaned the garage so you know I'm feeling pretty good. How I wish you could see me before I get much bigger, but I suppose that's wishing too much.

All my love, always

Peggy

P.S. Dr. Ehrenberg gave me Nov. 18th for baby's arrival. I didn't tell him we knew better. It has to be the 22nd.

I look forward to addressing your letters. It makes me so proud to write "Captain." Incidentally Bill Ballard left Wed. as a 1st Lieut. in Air Corps Supply at Miami Beach (training school I suppose).

[To George]
[Handwritten on 5/21/42, postmarked on 5/21/42 at 11:30 AM]
[From Greenwich, CT to Key West, FL]

Dearest George,

It's a misty, moisty morning and Mom and I are really lazy. I've been sleeping in the guest room with her and we've just had our breakfasts in bed and now she's reading the paper and I'm trying to get this off in the morning mail.

Everything's going fine here, except the gas rationing has made us stick pretty close to home. I did get to Round Hill on Tuesday to play 9 holes with Jeane. I shot a 58 which wasn't too bad, but poor Jeane was all over the course. After each shot I had to wait for her to take about 3. She's only played two years and this was her first time this year.

Yesterday Tina[32] and I cleaned the basement. What a mess you can't imagine. I'm sure the box for ashes from the fireplace had never been emptied before. We filled a barrel, 2 cartons, and an empty soap bag from the plant. These wood ashes are so dusty we were a sight. Then we burned all the

---

[32] Tina was hired to help with the children.

trash and the brush along the fence which Ryan has never cleaned up. So you should come and see how nice we look now.

I wish you could be here right now to see Larry. He just came in with his kitten. I got a tiger kitty from the nursery (Troy's) Tuesday and the children are ^crazy about him. He's under the bed now playing with Doxie's ball and Larry's refereeing with his head half under too. The only nuisance is Doxie. He's convinced the thing is another rat and its only excuse in this house is for him to exterminate it. I'm afraid the end will be quick and painful. I must say it looks like a rat, sort of so I can't blame him. Bill and Bernice came for dinner last night and Mom and I took them for 90¢ at bridge. The first hand we bid and made 6 spades. Have you been playing any?

Mrs. Alworth is in town and has asked Mother and me to have lunch with her Sat. I think we'll go into N.Y.C. tomorrow, Friday and stay all night—perhaps see a show. Mother's leaving Tuesday. I'll certainly miss her. It's too bad the weather hasn't been nicer. We've had several nice weeks though. I loved your letter and the reminiscences of Havana. We'll have so much more fun going next time.

What wonderful fun it will be going on trips after this is over. We'll appreciate everything a thousand times more.

The cat just ran in the closet and Larry climbed in after her yelling, "Pussy get out o dar." He picked her up and scrambled out.

Guess I better stop now and get Anna to put this in the box. The news is a little better these days. Do you think the Russians will hold out?[33] And the Chinese?[34]

We all miss Daddy very much especially Mama. What fun it will be when we're all together at last!!!

---

[33] Peggy is most likely asking for George's thoughts on the Second Battle of Kharkov, a fight between Soviet and Nazi forces in eastern Ukraine. The campaign began on May 12 and continued as a Soviet success until German airstrikes on May 15 stopped the Soviet advance. A German pincer attack cut off three Soviet forces from the rest of the front by May 22 and the Soviet troops trapped inside lasted six days before the offensive was called off. By May 30, the Soviet forces inside were either killed or captured. Only one in ten managed to escape (BEE 1998, 67).

[34] The latter half of the Second Sino-Japanese War overlapped with WWII. Once the U.S. declared war on Japan, China shortly followed, formally declaring war on the Axis powers. On May 15, the Imperial forces of the Japanese Empire occupied the areas of Zhejiang and Jiangxi, China, with the dual purpose of destroying air bases the American troops could use and defeating Chinese forces. The Japanese army also conducted searches for the American airmen who had parachuted out during the Doolittle Raid and conducted a retaliatory "reign of terror," destroying entire villages and murdering an estimated 250,000 Chinese civilians suspected of harboring or helping the American pilots (MUR 2000, 191). Miraculously 67 of the pilots and crewmen were aided by sympathetic Chinese and made it safely back to the United States (GRO 2005, 192).

I love you so very much and just count these days as lost without you.

All yours always
Peggy

[To George]
[Handwritten on 5/26/42, postmarked on 5/27/42 at 11:30 AM[35]]
[From Greenwich, CT to Key West, FL]

P.S. After writing this, I've finished one to Ki and Teedie. I guess it will be forwarded from Savannah.

Goodnight darling

Darling,

It seems as though I'm always feeling depressed for just having said goodbye to someone dear to me. I'm always the one that's left behind. Today it was Mother, two weeks ago it was Steppy, four weeks ago it was you, and so it goes month after month. Will it ever end satisfactorily? I wonder.

We spent a quiet day here in the yard with the children, and then I broke down and drove Mom to Harmon[36] in your car. It was a beautiful day and Larry went along to see "Grandma's Choo-choo." We put her on the Commodore at 5:20 and saw loads of trains and engines. Larry was so excited, he could hardly walk and waved at all the engineers. "Bye, Bye choo choo!"

---

[35] Postmarked May 27, 1942 at 11:30am and airmail postmarked May 28, 1942.

[36] Probably the Croton-Harmon train station.

We drove home and have just finished our dinner and find the house feels very lonesome, except for Doxie and the Kitten. Incidentally, they are getting along fine, now.

You were so sweet to call me last night. My birthday was as complete as possible without seeing you after that. I love my perfume and noted carefully the names of the brands you chose. I'm crazy about them both. Many thanks. I just don't know what to plan about coming down there. You know how anxious I am to see you at any possible time. It's really best for you to decide the advisability of my going, though. The expense is considerable and I don't know whether you'll be through there in two or three weeks or not. As far as health is concerned, it's O.K. I haven't any pep yet, but my stomach is better if I watch my diet. That should all clear up very soon. Now you write me what you think best and it's all settled. I can leave on an hour's notice. That's my custom by now.

After talking to you last night, I showed our wedding pictures to Mom, Marjorie, Bernice and Seeley and then the Sea Island ones. They were very polite and seemed to enjoy them and it made me feel as if you were right with me. How many happy memories we have! And how I'm learning to cherish them. All crowded into 4 years too. Last night Mom reminded me that our 5th anniversary is almost here and it just hit me that only four of those years we've lived together—4/5ths of our married life. Isn't that an awful thought with no sign of it resuming very soon?

Excuse the morbid thoughts. They only go to prove how much I love you and miss you every day and hate every minute we're kept apart.

My music teacher called today to say he had acquired an x card[37] for gas and would come out here if I'd resume my lessons. So I'm starting again Tuesday.

Mrs. Alworth is coming out next weekend with me. I'm a little disappointed as I miss a dance Sat. night at the Club, but I'll enjoy her as much, no doubt. She's asked me 4 times if you received a letter she wrote you. Did you?

Another reminder. Did you send Helen and Frank the case of turtle soup? When you have a chance send one collect to Mother and Dad addressed to Dad's office.

---

[37] "X" cards were given to people with high mileage jobs where the mileage could not be reliably estimated and who thus required the purchase of gasoline in unlimited quantities (NYT 04/23/1942, 16). A doctor or a traveling salesperson is an example of someone who might qualify for an "X" card.

Mother and I had a wonderful time in N.Y.C. We got in about noon on Friday and I took her to "Coq Rouge" for lunch and to [a] matinée "Priorities of 1942."[38] Then Ruth and Mac Black took us to [the] University Club for dinner and to see "Moon is Down."[39] We stayed at [the] Biltmore all night and had lunch Sat, at St. Regis with Mrs. Alworth. Came home and were in bed at 8:00 P.M.

I sent your radio down and ordered an indelible ink outfit sent to you with a stamp of your name for marking things. Let me know if they've arrived. Send Ki's address when you know it.

All yours always.

Peggy

XXXOO

---

[38] *Priorities of 1942* was a variety show organized by Clifford C. Fischer. It opened on March 12, 1942 and ran until September 6 of the same year at the 46th Street Theatre.

[39] *The Moon is Down*, a drama written by John Steinbeck (from the book of the same name), opened on April 7, 1942 and ran until June 6, 1942 at the Martin Beck Theatre.

[To George]
[Handwritten, possibly on 6/1/42]
[Locations unknown]

Dearest

This is one night you'll never regret not being with me. You should see, I'm in bed from poison ivy. It's in my ears, eyes, and on down. I've doused myself with P.A.L. for two days and although it does relieve the itching, it has turned me a spotted brown from all the iodine that's in it. A most attractive wife. The enclosed photo taken last week you had better cherish in case I fail to regain my normal color. It's even made my throat sore. Did you ever hear of anything so silly?

The most wonderful thing happened to me today. I received two letters from the most handsome Captain in the U.S. army, the most thoughtful, loving husband in the world, the most adored and badly missed Daddy there is and from the one I love most in all the world. Doxie received his pat and we had quite a talk about it. Larry promised to tell you loads of nursery rhymes and Georgia said "Daddy" and kissed your picture. "Whatchamacallit" gave me the first kick in the stomach! So it was a red letter day all around for your family because you were so nice as to write us _two_ letters.

Mrs. Allworth came out Saturday noon. I took her to Round Hill for lunch which she seemed to enjoy very much. Then we called on Mrs. Bigelow where she took us both last year. We came home and played with the children and Marjorie came up for dinner with us. We played gin rummy afterwards and went to bed early. Sun. a.m. Anna served our breakfast on the porch amidst children, kittens & Doxie. I took her to a noon train and really think she enjoyed the informality of a day at our house. She's an awfully good sport.

From the station I stopped at Marjories for Sun. lunch. Pete is out of town and she had the Ives, Buckhauts and Bowdens. Eddy Ives arrived in his white summer Navy uniform—a senior lieut. And just as much a blow hard as ever. I thought the navy would take a little of that out of him. Right now he _is_ the Navy. What a job I had keeping my mouth shut. As it was, I was so afraid I'd be nasty that I never said a word all afternoon. He discussed _his_ Navy as MacFarlane does _his_ shell plant, only far more dramatically. Even his wife addressed him as "Admiral" but he just loves it.

Tomorrow morning I'm taking Larry and Georgia and Tina to Mary Ward's. She's having a birthday party for Luke. It was supposed to have been today but it rained all day and still is now. They live right on the beach so the children are to play in the sand until lunch. Have lunch there then come home for naps. Larry's all excited about it except he wants to keep Luke's present for himself.

I'm supposed to play golf tomorrow with Jean and Helen Gorton but I'm afraid the poison ivy won't let me. Gosh! I'm glad you can't see me! I'm bad enough looking now without being spotted.

Nothing could please me more than to have you say you're losing your good disposition from being imposed on because of it. The Army is doing you a favor, Sir. And me too. Any other changes for the bad will be easy to overlook if that one good one is accomplished.

I've thought a good deal about adjustments after this is over and I fail to see that they'll be anything but fun. You can't worry me at all. You'll have new stories and experiences to make you an even more thrilling and interesting lover and I'll have a new baby that you won't hardly have even a prenatal acquaintance with.

Before closing I'll pass on an Alworth joke. On a radio quiz program a man was offered $128.00 if he'd answer truthfully a very intimate question that was professed to be difficult. He allowed he'd do his best. He was asked "What's the first thing your wife says when you get in her bed at night? Oh," said the man—"that's not hard." "Give the gentleman $128.00 boys," said the questioner.

I love you,
Peggy

[To Peggy]
[Handwritten on 6/15/42, postmarked on 6/15/42 at 6 PM]
[From Key West, FL to Greenwich, CT]

Darling:

That will be fine if you can get someone to come down here with you. You don't know how much I miss you dear. Yesterday, Sunday, I was wondering what you Georgia and Larry were doing. I sure would like to have been sitting out there on the lawn with you. Those few Sundays I did manage to get down from Groton[40] are certainly remembered as prizes.

Are you sure that it will be alright for you to travel down here? How do you feel? I do want to see you, but I don't want you to make the trip, if you feel it might upset you.

I can meet you up in Miami and I think that the best thing to do will be to rent a car up there to use while you are here. Then we could drive back down here together. I have checked on this and we can get a car alright.

Mr. Kingsley[41] writes me that he has two prospective buyers for 1941. I will let you know how this goes.

---

[40] George is probably referencing Groton, CT. In 1941 the United States Army Air Corps set up a training base at what is now the Groton-New London Airport. In early 1944 the airfield was turned over to the United States Navy.

[41] George Kingsley was an attorney in Minneapolis and Gillette family friend.

I would certainly like to spend one more Christmas there. But I suppose the only sensible thing to do is to sell it.

I had written 'Ki' but he had moved from one hotel to another. He said he finally got one of my letters.

Morrel just came back, a young Cuban officer[42] with him, just came up for the trip.

I am going to be very happy to see you, and am already looking forward to that drive back down along the keys. Perhaps we can spend the night in Miami.

With all my love
George

xxx Larry xxx for Georgia xxxxxx for Peggy

---

[42] Cuba declared war on the Axis powers in December 1941, following the Japanese attack on Pearl Harbor, and played an important role as a U.S. ally in WWII. Cuba's military gave the U.S. permission to build airfields and bases in Cuba to protect Caribbean sea lanes and the U.S. supplied Cuba with $7 million worth of modern military aircraft and up-to-date ships, equipment, and weapons for their Navy (NYT 03/05/1942, 4). During the war the Cuban Navy escorted hundreds of Allied ships through hostile waters, sailed hundreds of thousands of miles on convoy and patrol duty, and rescued over 250 U-boat victims from the sea (NYT 06/17/1942, 12). Many Cubans also served in the Allied forces and Cuban volunteers trained in the U.S. (NYT 07/13/1942, 3). In an effort to help the Navy, occasionally George and his team would take dispatches over to the American embassy in Havana, Cuba (STE 1991, 2).

[To George]
[Handwritten on a plain postcard, 6/16/42 at 11:30 AM]
[From Stamford, CT to Key West, FL]

Dear George

I haven't had a chance to write this week, but will try to do it tomorrow. We're all well. Mother is much better. Tina is on her vacation. I did the wash this morning and Larry and I picked wild strawberries this afternoon. Nan Miller is here and enjoyed them with me for dessert. We're now going to Stamford to the movies and I'll mail this. Mr. Denson (Greenwich) has a[n] old chest just like I want. Price $225. He's holding it 5 days for your O.K. I can manage to pay for it. Think I can make Key West Tues, June 30th.

Love
Peggy

[To George]
[Handwritten on a plain postcard on 6/17/42, postmarked on 6/17/42 at 11:30 AM]
[From Greenwich, CT to Key West, FL]

Dearest George

Again I haven't a letter written and the postman should be here any second. We're all fine, but it's raining again. I'm having an outdoor lunch Sunday for 40 people and will die if we have rain then. It's not much fun having a party without you. Doesn't seem to be any point to it. Larry just talked to you on his telephone. The bill was high "60¢" he said "for 15 min." It was about that long. He asked what you were doing and announced that you said you are "playing in the sand." I'm mailing you some new pictures of the children for your folder. Hope you like them. Let me know if you have a reservation for me Tues June 29th.

Peggy

[To George]
[Handwritten, possibly on 6/19/42[43]]
[Locations unknown]

Dearest George,

Here we are back at writing letters again. It seems so unsatisfactory after having you right with me for a few days. However, it's far better than nothing at all.

It's a shame your call came through late Wednesday night cause Larry and I had discussed all the things he was going to say. He wanted to send you a kiss and tell you to come and see him and Georgia real soon. Also "how was pussy" and that he was glad to have Momie back. The girls went out. I gave them bus fare to Greenwich and back and a movie thrown in. So Larry and I had supper together on the porch and we both climbed into my bed to wait [for] the ring. It rang 4 times before he fell asleep but each time he was saying "I want to talk to my Daddy" so loud that I could hardly find out what the person really wanted. If you

---

[43] According to the letter Peggy's father sent to George (and copied for Peggy), included in Additional Letters, he visited the family in Greenwich from Thursday the 16th to Sunday the 19th.

can get to call Sunday morning sometime about 9.00 that would be sure to find him here and awake.

Believe it or not after one night home my left breast is covered with that itching rash again. And tonight it looks as if Georgia has it on her legs. I'm so discouraged over it. I had just written a check today for $45.00 to pay for the previous treatments. Now I'm going to write Ehrenberg and see what he suggests. Maybe I'll have to move to Key West to get rid of it again.

Everything fine here otherwise except I haven't replaced Tony yet.

I had a swell visit with Dad. He phoned Thurs. a.m. from Wash. and got to Greenwich that night on the 10 P.M. express. Friday we sat on the porch all morning talking and playing with the children. They made a big fuss over Grandpa which of course pleased him no end. After lunch we went over to Round Hill. I borrowed Alph's shoes and clubs for Dad and what do you think he shot.—a 93— which is really good there for most fair golfers when they haven't played the course before. I had to blow up entirely and be miserable all the way around. I couldn't do a thing.

The Peters met us there for drinks which we toasted to you with great sincerity and then had a nice dinner out on the terrace. That was followed by a bridge game at the Peters which Daddy and I paid for.

Saturday morning was frightfully hot and humid (like Key West exactly) so we sat under the big tree very quietly except for Larry and Georgia jumping on Daddy's tummy on the blue chair and Doxie barking for someone to throw apples for him. We had lunch here and then Dad had to take the 1.42 to catch a train for Minneapolis. He said to send you his very best love when I wrote so here it is.

I've pasted the children's snapshots in our book today and found a few you haven't seen so am enclosing them. Also, an insurance bill from Marsh McClellan. I also found a large picture of the three of us for your folder. Be sure and take it out of the mount and slip it in.

Last night I went to Bill Wellington's to a buffet supper and bridge party. His married sister and brother-in-law were down from Boston and the Beanes and Hites were there. It was nice but after playing bridge 5 hours I was ready to come home. I mentioned to Alph that you might write him in regard to making a call on Casa Marina managers. He said he'd be only glad to.

It's been hot as hades here all day so Tina and I and the children haven't budged from the yard. Doxie is miserable. Right now I'm sitting at the dining room table in my night gown writing you and am still hot. The children can't seem to get to sleep it's so hot upstairs. Tina is preparing to go out. Tomorrow Edna Von Amerongen[44] is stopping on her way to L.I. from Westport with her 3 boys to have [a] picnic with us here. She stopped a few minutes on way up Sat.

As usual I miss you terribly and have a hard time attaching any importance to anything I do without you. All yours always

Peggy.

---

[44] This last name is possibly misspelled by the editor.

[To Peggy]
[Handwritten on 6/21/42, postmarked on 6/21/42 at 6 PM]
[From Key West, FL to Greenwich, CT]

Darling:

First, I love you very much. Five years ago today I was just as anxious to get home to marry you as I am now anxious to see you a week from Tuesday. My lovely, charming young lady is as fascinating to me today as five years ago, and far more necessary to me after the hard times she has helped me over and the many happy experiences we have shared. Sailing on Lake Windemere, tennis at the Manor House, Baron von Ribbentropp there too, the Chateau D'Ardennes; a blanket over our knees, champagne, moonlight and music on the terrace of the Schloss Hotel; Hungarian gypsy music in Budapest; Glofoda[45] Beach in Athens, the beautiful little valley of Gastadt; the visit to Agnes Drecoll shop, how I loved to see you in that black evening gown; the night in Forest Hills when you wore a beautiful nightie and surprised me so by saying, "Darling, I want to have a baby!", then one day in such a demure mood you sat on my

---

[45] Most likely a misspelling of Glyfada.

lap and told me I was going to be a daddy. And since then you have told me the same thing twice more! How naturally you seemed to know how to take care of a baby, and how proud and happy you have made me with two such children. I have just been looking at their pictures and wishing. And the pain and hard work they have brought you has been so uncomplainingly endured. Then I remember the gay evening we rode through the snow up to Trail Creek Cabin, the fun we had on Dollar Mountain, on the ice rink with Hans, then last spring our trip down to Hot Springs, and how pleased you were with a little sailfish pin. How charming and gracious you look in an evening gown, the beautifully managed home, the perfect little hostess at parties that everyone enjoys, and even envies a little bit, how you tempt me in a pretty nightie and the breath taking moments you have given me as you make me wait while you linger in taking it off, with the wonderful moments that follow when you lie in my arms with your lips to mine. How bravely you have met the War, carrying on without your husband. How you have hurried to comfort me when I lost my Father and then Jessie too. Those are a few of the things I think of when I say I love you.

Today I have been hoping it is nice weather up there in Greenwich for your lawn party. And I have been trying to picture our lawn, the roses, our friends scattered about talking and eating, Anna serving in her pleasant, well-mannered way. I wonder what you are wearing. I am sure everyone is having a good time especially two little guests who did not need a special invitation. Or perhaps they have gone over to play with Hodgie, Alph or the Bowdins.

A telegram just came from Larry and Georgia, tell them Daddy was very pleased and thank you dear. I will send it back in this letter so they can be sure I got it and see all five of us in the picture at the top.[46]

About coming down dear, as soon as you know let me know just what time and date you will arrive in Miami. Also let me know if you are going to have any gas left over on your ration card or mine. If so bring it down and we will get a hold of a car. If we can get enough gas we surely can rent a car in Miami and drive it down here. We would not use much driving around this little island, but it would be handy to have a car. I am trying to see if we can get a hold of a car in Key West and come down and back on the bus. That

---

[46] The Father's Day telegram enclosed is included below the letter.

is about 170 miles from Miami, and so would take about 20 gallons round trip. It would be fun to stay in Miami overnight. However, I am practically sure I can come up to meet you. I have made reservations for you at La Concha hotel.

Give Larry and Georgia a kiss for me, and as for you, well if you are real good you may have one when you get down here too.

> I love you dear,
> George (over)

[on the back]

Did I tell you before that there were two good prospects of selling our home. I hate to think of someone else living there, but I suppose it is the sensible move to make. However, this would make some difference in our plans to have you live out there. If you do think that you might want to go back down to Greenwich after the baby comes, it certainly will not cost us much more to keep the house for the balance of the lease, because of the state income tax when you move out to Minn. We can wait and see how that comes out anyway.

Father's Day Greeting *by* **WESTERN UNION**

GTG MPA116 15 SC=GREENWICH CONN

CAPT G R STEINER=

    CARE ARMY AIR CORP TROOP MEACHAM FIELD KEYWEST FLO=

HERE IS BIG HUG AND KISS TO SAY WE MISS YOU ON DADDYS DAY LOVE=

    LARRY AND GEORGIA.

I was very pleased to get this.

[To Peggy]
[Handwritten, undated[47]]
[Locations unknown]

Darling:

I was sorry to find this letter[48] back in our mail this morning. I mailed it Monday.

Your letter came with the mention that you might come down. Chances are, from the way things look now, that I will still be her[e] Sept 1. If I am I would sure like to have you come down. I will let you know of course if I hear anything about going back.

I love you just as much as I did Sunday

> *Love George (over)*
> *xxx Larry xxx Georgia XXX Peggy*

[on the back]
P.S. I will write you again tomorrow night.

---

[47] Possibly Wednesday, June 24 or July 1,

[48] One of George's letters to Peggy was returned to him. It was most likely his letter written Monday, June 15.

[To George]
[Handwritten on 7/24/42, postmarked on 7/24/42 at 4:30 PM]
[From Greenwich, CT to Key West, FL]

To the Dearest One in the World.

What a thrill I just had! Larry and Georgia and I are sitting out on the blue chair or rather I'm competing for it. Right now they and Doxie are all climbing in that tiny dog house door of the garage playing dog. The children are doing the barking. Doxie is just tagging along wagging his tail hoping they'll turn up an interesting smell. What I started to say was we heard the mailman's car and hurried down as fast as we could—being all bare-foot the driveway slowed us up a bit. We opened the box to see a new life[49] and several envelopes—Anna's [and] Tina's bills, advertisements, Grandma—but not Daddy. Then after reading what we thought was all—there was your letter after all and such a nice one too.

I'm glad to know what you did after I left you. It worried me to see you look that way. I'm going to be fine all through this. You provide everything possible to make me and

---

[49] A *Life* magazine.

the children happy except your own sweet self. But that being impossible now we'll surely have everything else. And soon we'll have an additional great blessing which you misunderstood me if you think I'm not as thrilled over as you are. It's just fun to tease you.

The heat has abated and Tuesday we were able to move again. Anna and I put up 6 quarts of string beans and wax beans and I made some really wonderful raspberry and currant jelly which actually came out right after the first cooking. Then I took Larry to Greenwich for a haircut and got him some new shoes and did the marketing. I also went to the Dr. and found my blood pressure O.K. likewise other tests. He's sure we're having another boy (should be our third boy from all predictions.) This breast trouble he attributed now to a pregnancy hormone deficiency. Our systems are funny things. If that's [what] it is evidently being with you made whatever gland it is work for that length of time. In Mother's letter this morning she said Thelma has the same thing and is also being treated for scabies. Both being pregnant it's pretty apt to be due to that condition instead of an [un]usual skin disease not likely that either of us would contact. I shall write her.

Larry just crawled up on the seat beside me and wants to know what each word is. He says, "Are you making Daddy?" "Are you making his feet now?" "Now, are you making Grandpa?" I[sn't] it funny the ideas they get? Doxie's lying under the chair and sends a tail wag and a lick.

Wednesday I took the children and both girls to the beach. We took the boat out and how they all loved it! It was a bit too public for Momie. Larry would delight you with his enthusiasm for the water. I'm also teaching him the different birds and flowers and he's doing remarkably well. Just now he heard a Katydid (big beetle) and said "Hush up Katydid—I don't want any more rain. About a week ago I told him when they make that noise with their wings they were asking for rain.

Wednesday night I talked to the girls about going to Mlps and miracle—they accepted! I can't tell you how relieved I am. So now as we hoped I'll leave here about Oct. 1st and be back Jan. 1st. If you can only get to Mlps. Christmas. I've still to find someone to stay here. Marj. MacCagney is going to Chapel Hill N.C. to be with Mac.

Yesterday I washed both cars, used the hose on the

garage, weeded my garden, and painted the 'taylor tot' and 'wheel barrow' for #3. Then I dressed and went to Bowdens for dinner. Peters, Hites, Beanes, Bill Wellington were there. Played bridge after. Never had bid all night. Today I'm playing golf with Bill Bowden, Pete and Ges Hite. No need to tell you I[m] scared to death after being so lousy with Dad last time. Having dinner with Peters tonight. Tomorrow I'm going to cocktail party at Ives and dinner at Adams so you see this is quite a busy weekend. All I can think of is what fun it all could be if the war were over and you were here. I just read Hull's speech[50] and thought it an excellent statement of the aims and hopes of the ultimate peace. If the world could only be forced to take such an unselfish program to put into practice.

The children are getting impatient with my letter writing so I[ll] give them a little rough house!

---

[50] Peggy is referencing Secretary of State Cordell Hull's speech delivered on July 23, 1942 entitled, "What America is Fighting For." In his speech Hull says Americans, "are fighting today because we have been attacked [and need] to preserve our very existence." Hull suggests, "with victory achieved, our first concern must be for those whose sufferings have been almost beyond endurance." He then speaks of cooperation among nations to aid in the transition from wartime to peacetime, economic strategies to promote trade and growth of industry, and cautions against "extreme nationalism," a direct contributor to the present war. The speech transcript and a recording of Hull reading it, can be found on archive.org by searching, "What America is Fighting For."

All yours always
Peggy

Larry's Kiss

[To Peggy]
[Handwritten on 8/9/42, postmarked on 8/12/42 at 6 PM]
[From Key West, FL to Greenwich, CT]

Give Mrs. Peake a ring and see where Rob is.

My very favorite girl,

Your picture is here in front of me with a darling little girl on your lap and the sweetest little boy sitting next to you. The thrilling part to me is to know that they are our children. How much I would like to be having Sunday evening supper with you out on our porch. Afterwards I would help you clean up, then we would go in the living room to play a game of backgammon at which I would surely win. You are always the best company in the world. And I long for a bit of that company.

There still are rumors about our going back, but first they will have to send someone down to relieve us. Several of the sections which came down from Manchester at the same time we did are on their way back now.

A big surprise. Don Morrell got married last week to he says, "a very charming young lady." She was a stewardess on one of the air lines. He is all beaming and happy as anything. He is really a swell fellow. He always asks about you when he comes in. He made me a present of a bottle of rum yesterday when he got back from Cuba.

I have not heard a word from Gil or Aunt Dell, if I had their address I would write. Why don't you drop them a line and find out how everything went. I thought Gil was coming down here for sure.

I was over swimming most all afternoon. It was a swell day and the water just right. That is the best thing down here on a hot afternoon, nothing could feel much better than diving off the end of that dock. Stretched out on the float with a gentle breeze blowing I wished and wished I had my pretty wife out there with me.

I had a nice letter from 'Ki.' He and Teedie are settled now. They found a nice apartment in Springfield, Ohio which is about 18 miles from Wright Field. Their address is 1802 Overlook Drive. The phone is 2-8934 which might be well to jot down so we have it up there. Mary Olson has gone down there to work for them and Mary's son and daughter in law are living over at 1941 Knox to look after the house. When you get ready to go out there I think it would be well to let Nell and Mary know before hand as they will be very glad to have the house opened up and things ready for you.

I love you and miss you so much my darling. I know I have the nicest girl in the world. All my love dearest.

Yours, George

[To Peggy]
[Handwritten on The Columbus stationary, postmarked 8/28/42 at 1 PM]
[From Miami, FL to Greenwich, CT]

Darling:

Wish I had my hair cut before you left. I stopped in a barber shop on the way back and I sure needed one. I had quite a talk with the barber who came from Salerno, Italy on the Bay of Naples. We stopped there remember. He believed in state socialism when I went in, (but thought Mussolini and Hitler were terrible).[51] I hope I changed his mind.

The room looks awful empty now without Momie sitting here knitting and Larry looking out at the pigeons, boats, trucks and airplanes.

I am going to go over and buy a new blouse, get some golf balls, Leica film, and then catch the one o'clock bus for Key West.

I sure enjoyed our visit and hope we will be together soon. I love you very much.

---

[51] The parentheses are the editor's addition to clarify that George was not hoping to change the man's mind about Hitler and Mussolini, but only about state socialism. In future letters as George expresses himself, it is clear that he supports neither dictator nor their policies.

XXX Georgia XXX Larry XxXxx Momie

    My love,
      George

Tell Larry I will feed the pigeons for him before I leave. I am thinking about you on the train

[To Peggy]
[Handwritten on The Columbus stationery, probably written and postmarked the same as the previous letter]
[From Miami, FL to Greenwich, CT]

Darling:

Just want to let you know how good a time I had with my dear wife and little boy. You were so sweet to bring him down.

This war will all be over before too long then you will be doing all your travelling with me.

I love you so much dear, and am very happy about our new baby

All my love,
George

[To George]
[Handwritten, probably on 8/31/42, postmarked 8/31/42 at 11:30 AM]
[From Greenwich, CT to Key West, FL]

Darling,

I'm writing on my breakfast tray after having Anna's first meal in over a month. My! It was good to see her smiling face coming through the door this morning. At the moment I had both children and Doxie in bed with me. The latter was an accident. He got over jealous and just had to join the fun.

I waited here all day yesterday for you to phone. It worries me a little, but I suppose you got tied up. I certainly hope you got back without any mishap.

After mailing the note to you in Jacksonville, Larry and I had quite an exciting day. A Negro girl in a nurse's uniform knocked on the door and asked if the little girl she had could play with Larry for a while. She said her mother was asleep in the next compartment and I could call her if I needed her. At that the nurse disappeared and I never saw her again. She was the train stewardess and wanted to get rid of the child. Anyhow, the little girl was about Larry's age, quite a bit larger but manageable. She spoke mostly Spanish which annoyed Larry at first, but they played and roughhoused all afternoon and got on beautifully. I put two pillows on the floor in the front of the john and they would climb on the john and jump off and chase each other squealing down to the men's room where they swung around on the curtain and came back. Everyone on the train knew them, but I had no complaints. It got to be 8.00 P.M. and nobody had come for the child so I rang for the porter and asked him to tell the mother that I was taking them both for supper. We got a table for four and they both ate like angels so all would have been fine, but a Canadian girl arrived with a six month old child to take the fourth seat. She couldn't eat her dinner as the child wriggled, so I ended up holding her baby while she ate. We got back to the compartment. Still no sign of the Mother. So I bathed Larry and got him to bed and asked the porter to get the child's bed things and I'd get her ready too. At that, the mother came in barefooted in the most immodest chiffon negligee. She was on her way to N.Y.C from Santo

Domingo[52] where she had just received word that her husband had been killed in a crash over Dieppe[53]. He was a flight commander (British). The poor girl had lost two sisters in the bombing of London[54] and had nobody left. She had left there 5 months ago and gone to Lisbon where she took the clipper to Santo Domingo. The poor thing was beside herself naturally and the child was too much for her. I got her to bed and just as I was leaving she said with more bitterness than I've ever heard before "And what do you think, they're sending me the D.S.O."[55] That would be adding insult to injury.

---

[52] Probably Santo Domingo, Dominican Republic.

[53] The Dieppe Raid (also called Operation Jubilee) took place on August 19, 1942 in the German-occupied French port of Dieppe. Designed with the dual purpose of appeasing Stalin who was clamoring for a second front in France to take the pressure off of Soviet troops and as an experiment to see how easy or hard it would be to land on the French coast, the results were disastrous (GRO 2005, 389). Over half of the men in the British, Canadian, and American forces who made it over (the overwhelming majority of those were Canadian) were killed or taken prisoner and the resulting Axis victory made it clear to the Allies that an invasion of France would take more time and planning than originally thought (SMI1 2008, 560n-561n).

[54] The Blitz began with the daytime bombing of civilian targets in London on September 7, 1940. It lasted until May 1941. London was bombed at one point for 57 consecutive nights, leaving 10,000 dead and more than 50,000 injured (SMI1, 482). By November 1940, the Blitz had expanded to include bombing raids against other British cities and towns (BRI1 2003, 161).

[55] The DSO, or Distinguished Service Order, was awarded for exemplary service by officers of the British Armed Forces (initially including the Commonwealth) during wartime.

After that I went into the Canadian girl's compartment and heard her story which was equally interesting, but if this is going in the morning mail I'll have to skip that.

Larry and I got home on time without mishaps. We got Bitty Hite to bring the car to [the] station and were home by twelve in pouring rain, of course. It rained all day and night. Yesterday, it rained all morning so we stayed in [the] play room. We did get out after the naps for a while. Today, is starting out fine. I haven't called anyone yet so guess I'll try and get a golf game.

Larry has been bubbling over to Tina about you and Key West. The sailboat ride seemed to be the most important.

Georgia is wonderful. Jabbers all the time, but no one knows what half of it is.

All yours darling
Peggy

P.S. I'll let you phone me as I have to make a call person to person

[To George]
[Handwritten, undated[56]]
[Locations unknown]

My darling Peggy,

It really was hard to hang up last night. I got such a thrill out of hearing your dear voice. It was raining and blowing very hard last night. I came right back to my hut, looked at some pictures of you, then went to bed to think about you until I fell asleep.

I have some snapshots here on my desk now. Several of you holding Larry with the Buick behind you in Forest Hills. He is such a sweet looking little fellow and you look so pretty with that pleased proud look you are giving him. Then there is the one of you sitting on the lawn with Georgia on your lap while she holds a teddy bear. I like that one you took of Larry and myself on the way back to Miami. I am more than fortunate to have such a handsome little boy, such a pretty little girl, and to be married to such an attractive young lady. The truth is darling I just love you more all the time.

---

[56] This letter has been placed at the end of August 1942 but could easily have been written at some point in September or October of the same year.

And I am getting awful anxious to see our new baby.

I have not had any word yet from Manchester on my revised orders. I was disappointed about not driving up as I had planned on stopping overnight in New York, coming home for the night, and picking up the convoy on the parkway the next day. However it works out I am planning on seeing you within a week.

Col. Merrick[57] has put in a request that I be transferred to Miami together with the men I have down here. Several of them have come to me saying that if I get transferred they would like to stay with me. Anyway they are all very satisfied with the job we have done down here. As soon as I hear whether we are to stay in Miami or go back up to Manchester I will let you know.

I just have to tell you again how very much I love you my dear. If we could only spend the evening together.

I noticed an article in Readers Digest which I thought might interest you as you like those little Porcelain figures. I cut it out and will enclose it.

---

[57] Colonel L.M. Merrick of the I Bomber Command, assigned to the First Air Force during this time.

Also I am sending you a paper which Miss Finn would like to have signed by you in the presence of a notary public and two witnesses. Mr. Kingsley wanted this done so that Ki and I would have equal rights in this cemetery lot. Sorry to trouble you with this. I will enclose an addressed envelope for you to return this paper to Miss Finn.

I had dinner with Ginny Street Monday night over at the officers club. The meal was excellent, we had to wait about 45 minutes for a table so you can see they are well patronized. She is still waiting for Gordon, and now has a job filing in the Navy Purchasing department. She says the work is dull, but keeps her busy, and then she has made a lot of friends among other Navy wives and young officers at the sound school. It was one of those beautiful moon light nights, so she wished very much that Gordon were there, and as for me, well I just keep telling myself this war cannot last forever.

Just got a letter from Ki. He is down in St. Louis at some Air Corps procurement school for several weeks. Teedie went home for a week then came back to St. Louis.

Will write you again tomorrow.

I miss you so much my dear.

    With my love
        George (over)

[on the back]

You do not have to sign the affidavit just enclose it with the Quit Claim Deed which is the one you will sign.

I just want to tell you again I love you very much.

[To George]
[Handwritten, possibly on 8/31/42, postmarked 9/2/42 at 11:30 AM]
[From Greenwich, CT to Key West, FL]

Darling,

I found some cactus needles[58] in Greenwich today and I'm sitting here at the desk listening to—I'll bet you've guessed already—the Hungarian Gypsy music. It brings back so many memories of you and balmy summer evenings driving [the] Buick down dark Austrian and Hungarian roads with lights only now and then from wayside shrines where someone had stopped to put a candle. Then the gayety of Budapest with restaurant lights on the water of the Danube and you pouring me some wine while the violinists played that wonderful minor harmony.

After writing you this morning I got up and picked at least a dozen beautiful tomatoes from our bushes and tried to get the flowers in order. Nobody seems to looks at them when I'm not here. Larry and Georgia played beautifully together all morning. They seem so happy to see each other that they haven't hardly had a fight since we returned.

---

[58] Cactus needles were used on old phonographs.

I met Chloe and Jean at the new Howard Johnsons for lunch after doing my marketing. Then Jeane and I played 9 holes of golf and had a ginger beer. I beat her 9 up with a 56. So whatchamacallit didn't hinder me too much.

Barbara Miller's wedding announcement came in the mail this morning. She and Dick were married last Tuesday. He's already in [a] Texas camp according to letters from Mother which arrived at the same time.

Mother's letter also had bad news of Ford[59]. From some passengers off the Gripsholm[60] a passage came through the papers of the atrocities of Japs on American prisoners saying [the] two receiving [the] worst treatment were Floyd Bennett owner of Manilla Bulletin and Ford Wilkins his

---

[59] H. Ford Wilkins, Peggy's cousin to whom she was very close, was in Manila when the Japanese captured the city in January 1942. Ford was working as a New York Times and CBS correspondent in the Philippines and was the editor of the Manila Bulletin (NYT 10/25/1983, 34). The paper was also known as the Manila Daily Bulletin (GLU 2005).

[60] The MS Gripsholm was a Swedish ocean liner with the distinction of being the first ship built for transatlantic express service powered by diesel instead of steam (MIL 2008, 99). Initially a passenger ship used for back and forth travel across the Atlantic, from 1942-1946 the United States chartered it to make exchanges and repatriations. The ship carried Japanese and German nationals to exchange points at neutral ports where American, Canadian, and Latin American citizens were picked up (MIL 2008, 103). Peggy is referring to the Gripsholm's first voyage from New York to Portuguese-controlled Mozambique, retuning to New York on August 25, 1942. A number of exchanged prisoners published their experiences at the hands of the Japanese, outraging the American public with not only text and speeches, but graphic images (MIL 2008, 105).

editor.[61] This was due to the fact that they refused to spread Jap propaganda as ordered and were thrown into a Spanish dungeon. When I told Bernie that over the phone this morning, she said "well, I think he was pretty foolish not to do as they asked. After all no American would ever know or blame him if they did."

The gypsy music is over and I must get to bed. Thanks for your note from the Columbus.[62] It is awful to go back to a room that's empty when it's been so full only a few minutes before. Someday I hope we'll never have to leave one without both going at once and then only in the same direction.

I'll go up to that cold old bed now and dream of one I was in not but a week ago which might have been too warm for some, but it suited us fine.

Yours always
Peggy

---

[61] Ford was picked up by the Japanese and interned at the Santo Tomas internment camp in Manila on January 6, 1942. His later testimonies detail the torture and severe mistreatment of not only himself and Mr. Bennett, but of the other prisoners as well (WIL 1945, 2).

[62] The Columbus Hotel in Miami, Florida. The first page of George's letter, written on hotel stationery, is included in Memories.

[To George]
[Handwritten, probably the 9/2/42, postmarked 9/1/42 at 11:30 AM[63]]
[From Greenwich, CT to Key West, FL]

Darling:

Larry and Georgia have just pattered off my bed to the playroom for their breakfast. What a going over I get these mornings! How I'll manage with three I don't know. You'll be home to cope with that, thank goodness. My big tummy is so tempting to play horsey on that it's a wonder if #3 isn't born cantering.

Yesterday I spent with my sewing machine. It was a nice day so Anna and Tina brought it down on the porch for me and I all but finished a pair of flannel pajamas for Larry. I've made Georgia a dress on it since I got back too.

When I went to market Mon. I forgot to tell you a girl who looked familiar to me came up and spoke. I couldn't place her and then she said "I'm Ginna Brown." In a minute Tim came in and we had quite a chat over the A & P meat counter. He was in civilian slacks which seemed to rankle me a bit. I don't suppose it should. Anyhow, they've

---

[63] This letter is possibly in the wrong envelope as the postmark date precedes the date it was written.

taken over his family place here in Greenwich which has been empty some time and are living just off of No. Maple Ave. They asked all about you and your activities since Bill Hause's wedding and both sent their best when next I wrote you. They are just getting settled now so I'll have them up shortly.

This morning I'm hoping to get an appointment for my hair. I still have the salt water in it. It's a nice day again and I hate to waste the time but there's a dance at Round Hill Friday and I'd like to look as well as possible. I'm also going to try and give Georgia a birthday party that day instead of Sat.

We've got $100.00 in our account for the 2nd honeymoon. Isn't that exciting?

Larry just marched in with the paper rolled up under his arm. So here goes for my dose of medicine today.

All my love always
Peggy

 — Kiss from Larry X X from Lee

[To George]
[Handwritten, possibly written on 9/3/42]
[Locations unknown]

Darling,

This is a beautiful warm sunny morning, how I wish you could be here to share it with me and the kids and perhaps have a golf game and swim. If they had only ordered you out of there now for a better place near home!

I've had my breakfast and just finished knitting Larry a green cap to match his pants you watched me labor on. It looks so cute on him. Yesterday I did manage to get my hair done and it looks and _feels_ quite differently. Then I went to Allison Flaccus's for lunch. She had 10 girls and it was very nice. They have the most beautiful new house it just made me jealous to look at it. Their property is on a little secluded lake about three miles out of Greenwich and their house sits between that and a high hill of tall pines in the rear. You'd never know there was another house for miles around. The house itself is large and rambling with all sorts of cute screened porches and wrought iron railings. Its white shingled on the outside with green blue blinds and the most fascinating maroon front door. They have four children so it's a little bigger than we need, but we could come pretty close to filling it up. What fun we are going to have if we ever build or own a home all our own.

Last night I was knitting and playing Dvorak's New World Symphony when the phone rang & it was mom and dad. They are fine and wanted to know all about you and sent their love. Mom sounded pretty low over Ford. I wish I could think of something to say in a letter to Aunt Mary and Uncle Tim.[64] Any other news would be easy to send sympathy over. If you care to write it's H. F. Wilkins, Babson Park Florida. If he's dead I hope he died quickly.

Don't you feel pretty proud of yourself for having played a part in curbing the Atlantic sub sinkings?[65] The papers these last few days are really encouraging along that line at least.

Guess I'd better say goodbye for today. Anna's after me

---

[64] Ford's parents were Dr. Timothy Wilkins and his wife Mary, Peggy's aunt on her mother's side.

[65] By June 1942, German submarines had destroyed nearly 5 million tons of Allied shipping. The German naval presence in the Atlantic was so detrimental to the U.S. that the Interlocking Convoy System was developed. Sonar, air escorts, and voice radio communications, and special rescue ships made up the convoys (EB n.d.). The convoy system was so effective that by mid-July 1942, the Germans were forced to move their submarines away from the Atlantic Coast of the U.S. (BRI 2003, 77).

to plan Georgia's party tomorrow. I have Hodgie, 2 Beanes, 2 Wards, Wendy Ballard and Anne Bowden coming. It's not going to be fancy but if it's a nice day, they will have a good time.

You should have seen Larry & Georgia on the teeter-totter under the apple tree yesterday. They had a real squealing good time. They found by sitting flat on the ground when their respective ends came down that the other was suspended helpless in the air. The only hitch was if Larry left Georgia too long she would deliberately fall off. It was a good fall too, but she'd get up and make him let her on again.

All our love again
Peggy.

[To Peggy]
[Handwritten, postmarked 9/5/42 at 6 PM]
[From Key West, FL to Greenwich, CT]

Dearest Peggy,

That picture the soldier took of us just before you left the first time you were down is on my desk. I like your expression and the way your arm is put through mine. It is nice to have a wife you can be proud of, not only an attractive little girl to have on your arm, but a charming lady to talk with, so capable in running a beautiful home, the mother of such fine children, and one that loves me very much.

I got a real thrill yesterday when I got two letters on the same day from the one I like most to get letters from.

There has not been very much doing here since you left. The 80th Bomb has been keeping 2 planes here since then which means there are six other officers here for company. So we have gone to the Ocean View for a good steak dinner and stopped in to the Officers Club for drinks. They are a nice lot of young fellows and it is good to have them here.

There was one in particular who I enjoyed talking with, a Lt. Norton. He was interested in the history of these old forts which led to the Civil War, then to a comparison of the Civil War fighting with the present, and then to the economic and political causes of the war and the possible means of preventing future wars. He had some interesting ideas on handling men with incidents from his own experience and from history to illustrate them. It is very pleasant to find someone who has interesting thoughts to talk about, rather than the common line of chatter. This boy had enlisted as a private, been appointed to West Point, spent a 3 month summer vacation with naval cadets aboard a battleship during fleet gunnery practice, graduated, [w]ent to Kelly Field[66] and trained a year for pilot.

I sure miss you and Larry now that you are gone. But it was [a] real pleasure having you here. Now I am getting mighty interested in seeing Georgia. Today she is two years old. I'll bet her proud Mama has her all dressed and looking mighty cute. But how long she will stay dressed up I would not care to guess. I hope she grows up to be just exactly like her Momie.

I got your letter written from the train. Wish I could have been riding up there with you.

---

[66] Kelly Field, located at the Kelly Air Force Base in San Antonio, Texas.

Maybe I will be home for Georgia's next birthday, let's hope so, cause I like birthday cake.

My love dear,

George.

← That's for Larry and tell him to see if he can make as pretty a one for me.

[To George]
[Handwritten, possibly on 9/7/42]
[Locations unknown]

Darling,

This has been a holiday so they say. I don't suppose you
knew it either. Betty Bowden came up here this afternoon
and is staying overnight with me. We sat out in the sun until
it got chilly and were entertained by Larry and Georgia
turning somersaults. Generally Georgia has to have a push
from behind by Larry after she gets her head down, but
today she finally did it alone. Not only alone but without
using either hand. One was clasped tightly around a teddy
bear and the other a blade of grass. She was so delighted
you'd think she'd learned to fly. She had on a blue dress
Mother sent her for her birthday and was she a picture?
The dress just matched her eyes and then a blue ribbon in her
blonde curls and blue socks. Of course usually she was
bottoms up with only pants showing, but occasionally you
could get a glimpse of what ought to be.

Your phone call yesterday morning thrilled us all. Larry
was just like me. After we hung up he thought of so many
things to say to Daddy and couldn't see why we didn't call

right back and tell you. A few minutes after our visit I took the two of them and walked up to the farm. It was a lovely cool Sept. morning and I thought of other walks we'd all had together up that drive and wished so you could be there. We stopped to watch the baby pigs fed and squealed along with them. Then up to see the chickens—no turkeys this year. Then the cows and then Doxie chased a big cat up a tree and was thoroughly scolded by Miss Georgia. She's taken upon herself all of Doxie discipline and it's something to hear, but better to see the stern expression on her face.

We ran into Mr. Hekma a little further on and had a nice visit. I said I'd heard from his daughter-in-law and that she didn't think she could live here while we're gone. He said he was afraid Frank wouldn't be back all along and thanked me for the offer. Also said they'd keep close watch on the house if we had to leave it empty.

I did get to the club for dinner yesterday noon with [the] Beanes and Bouscarens. Then played 18 holes of golf with Alf. in a 2 ball much needed foursome. We came in second too with a 69 (combined handicap 28). After that we all went to a supper party at the Cluett's where I was high winner at poker ($5.75). I'm proud of that cause they are all experienced players.

Betty's getting restless so I'll stop for tonight.

All my love as ever
Peggy XXO

[To Peggy]
[Handwritten on 9/7/42, postmarked on 9/9/42 at 11:30 AM]
[From Key West, FL to Greenwich, CT]

My darling,

You have sure kept me happy with letters, so often and so nice too. I could hardly believe when I got another one today. It was the one telling about your trip back to Greenwich. Peggy is always doing something nice for somebody else. All those sweet, considerate things you do, always in such a matter of fact way, are just one more reason for loving you. It is those thoughtful acts that brighten the rough spots in the world.

Now you are going to have to tell me the Canadian girl's story. When you realize how many thousands of times those bitter, personal tragedies are being repeated it brings some realization of the horrible affair this war is.

Your stories about Larry and Georgia, like the one on the teeter-totter always get read over several times and thought of many times with a smile. Give them both a big kiss and tell them it was sent special in a letter from daddy.

A couple of Majors and a Colonel were down from the Air Force in Miami yesterday and again this evening. They had been told what a terrible place Key West is, but were quite outspoken in their satisfaction at the way their planes and crew are being taken care of, and expressed their thanks for what we are doing here. That helps a lot.

They had some business down in the Navy yard yesterday, so I arranged to show them all through one of the submarines, showed them around the harbor defenses, the town, the Naval Air Station, and then they took me to dinner at Vera Belles. They all seemed quite interested in the history of Key West and these old forts.

After spending all day with them yesterday I took a break today, played golf (quite well too) even had a caddy, then went swimming. There were some youngsters 8-10 years old swimming off the float who wanted me to dive and swim with them, it just made me think how much fun we have ahead of us with Larry and Georgia. Golly with one more it looks like poor old Dad will be in for some duckings when we go swimming.

This evening I sat out on the sea wall with the two pilots and navigator just talking about school experiences and families at home. They are such decent clean cut young American boys I sure hope that when the war is over that the real power and authority in our country is taken over by this type of people. All three of them are married and each one went out of the way to tell what a really swell girl he had married. If they have as nice wives as they say they must be just about half as nice as mine.

Next letter I will write in a location with our prearranged method and you see if you can pick it out.

Don't forget those pictures I want printed will you. Also you had better include Meacham Field in the address on letters, as some of yours have been sent over to the Navy and to Key West Barracks before I get them.

Thanks again for the letters I will try to keep up my end.

Wish you were in my arms right this minute.

Love, George

[To George]
[Handwritten, possibly on 9/9/42]
[Locations unknown]

Dearest,

If you could look out of our bedroom window this morning you'd think winter had come for sure. The wind is blowing and it's raining and very dark. We're all very cozy, however. The children are fighting over who gets the last baking powder biscuit and I'm in bed full of breakfast and have a good book to read when I finish saying good morning to you.

Betty Bowden stayed until about noon yesterday. We sat and knitted most [of] the morning as it rained yesterday too. I feel sorry for her, but she does have a disagreeable disposition born from a terrific inferiority complex. She always comes up here unable to say anything but yes and no, but after a few hours she's very interesting and pleasant company. She'd make someone a darn good wife if he'd treat her kindly and on the level. She needs a man like I have, but then most people would like you. I suppose I'm selfish to want you all to myself when there isn't another in the world for any other girl. Just like Doxie. You two have no equals in the Kingdoms of dog and man.

Your nice letter came yesterday and now we already have enough money for a very fancy skiing weekend. Isn't that thrilling to dream about.

What do you think of your wife throwing a party tomorrow night at Round Hill? I'd planned to have it at home but somehow it just seemed too much trouble without having you to do it for. The occasion is the Bouscarens are moving to Chicago next week and I am so fond of Chloe I wanted to do something. I really will miss her more than anyone. Thurs. night they have a dinner dance so it should be fun. I've invited the Hites, Adams, Turbells, Beanes, Linens, Bouscarens and I'm trying to get Robbie Peake to come. I left the message with Dave yesterday but haven't heard yet. I do hope he can make it so I can get you all the news and also I'd love to see him myself. We had a nice talk on the phone Mon. night. He's fine and has a week leave (darn it! Why can't you). I gave him all our family news and your address. He said he'd write very soon.

I read the President's speech[67] yesterday morning and have been mad ever since. He cracked down on the farm bloc[68]

---

[67] Peggy is referring to Roosevelt's Fireside Chat #22, better known as his Labor Day speech, delivered on September 7, 1942, titled: *On Inflation and Food Prices*.

[68] The Farm Bloc refers vaguely to a group of Congressional representatives who have banded together to seek legislation that benefits or protects the agricultural industry. In

but why doesn't he dare even so much as mention labor, its strikes, and traitors? At least he got Congress mad. I hope they come across with a real bill freezing both farm prices and wages. They probably don't dare with elections coming up.

The only thing is that winter will come again to Russia. I still can't believe poor Stalingrad will hold, but at least Hitler can't finish the Russian armies this fall.

Roosevelt's speech he explains that the cost of living is rising because Congress exempted most farm products used for food and clothing from the freeze on the cost of living other commodities like rent and services experienced. He calls this exemption "an act of favoritism" and insists that unless the cost of food is controlled, workers will have to see a wage increase in order to survive. Roosevelt informs the public that he has told Congress they have until October 1 to pass legislation allowing him the authorization to stabilize the cost of living, including the price of farm commodities. He continues with a veiled (and then not-so-veiled) threat of an executive order if Congress fails to act, arguing that this is an example of total war (or war all over the world) and executive power is even more important than usual. He says this total war will cost the country nearly one hundred billion dollars in 1943, thus people must stop spending money on luxury items.

Roosevelt also suggests Congress put a floor under the farm products' prices in addition to the ceiling he had requested so that post war the country would see neither inflation nor a crash in farm prices and wages. Near the end of his speech, he once again reminds the public, "And wars are not won by people who are concerned primarily with their own comfort, their own convenience, their own pocketbooks."

Peggy is upset upon having her family's loyalty and actions questioned, as the sacrifices and struggles of the remaining farmers (especially the small farms) and farm industry as it is converted to war production, are completely overlooked in this speech. Included in Additional Letters is a letter to George from Peggy's father, discussing the challenges and sacrifices made by the agricultural machinery industry as they transition to wartime production.

A transcript of Roosevelt's speech as well as a recording of Roosevelt delivering it can be found at millercenter.org by searching "Fireside chat #22."

I can't tell you what a relief it was to know there are some officers down there and particularly one who you enjoyed. I do so hate to think of you spending your evenings all alone.

My love to you dear.
Peggy

[To George]
[Handwritten, probably also written on 9/9/42]
[Locations unknown]

Darling,

I hope you aren't getting tired of this continued line of chatter that I'm sending you every day and here it is twice today, but this is really tomorrow's letter.

You really should know how much I miss you right now though. It's rained all day and not even the children got out. Larry and I did don our raincoats for a quick trip to Congers and Banksville for food but that's all. I knitted, sewed and read. We all washed Doxie. Larry and Georgia perched themselves on the laundry stools and watched while Momie scrubbed and Doxie groaned. Georgia was very worried about it all and gave me reprimands at all points saying "Momie, stop it. Poor Doxie." Then I started some grape jelly. It's just in juice form tonight and reminded me of Welch's grape juice and you.

How I wish I could send this to you. It's even better. Maybe I'll get a half bushel more and put up just the juice.

Larry had supper with me and then I lit a fire in the

grate and we pulled up your big chair and had the 3 bear story before he went to bed. The girls went out and the children to sleep so Doxie and I are left all alone in front of the fire. I just finished my bills and am in the midst of combing Doxie wishing you were here to lie in front of the fire with us. Somehow you belong with a gratefire in my mind. Perhaps it's because you both are so warm and comfortable to be with. Doxie looks beautiful. I got out a peck of old hair and it's hardly half. He's all curly and smells good for a change. On the table beside me is a pretty vase of flowers from our garden. They are yellow marigolds, lavender cosmos and lavender scabiosa. I know you'd love them too.

Tomorrow I'm going to Red Cross all day and my dinner is tomorrow night. I still haven't heard from Robbie.

I'm enclosing a nice letter from Dad.

I love you very very much
Peggy

[To Peggy]
[Handwritten, possibly on 9/9/42, postmarked 9/11/42 at 11:30 AM]
[From Miami, FL to Greenwich, CT]

My darling Peggy:

We are beginning to get a bit of rain down here now. There are quite a lot of storms but they do not always hit us, you can see them off in the distance while the sun will be shining here. I guess they do not spread over as wide an area as up home there because I do not often remember of seeing storms and not being in them except down here. Almost every night even though it is [a] clear star light night, you can see lightning flashing in several directions.

Last evening I went up with one of the B-18's[69] for a while.

---

[69] It is possible that George is in a B-18B. B-18 bombers (built by the Douglas Aircraft Company) had been around since the late 1930s but were quickly replaced by more useful bombers like Boeing's famous Flying Fortress. Most B-18s were obsolete by the time the war began, however, they were the most numerous bomber deployed outside the continental U.S. (FRA 1988, 191). After Pearl Harbor, the bombers were incorporated into Sea Search and Attack (SSA) Squadrons where they were used in a defensive capacity to protect against U-boat attacks (FRA 1988, 191). In 1942, 122 B-18As were modified to B-18Bs to help combat the U-boat threat off American shores. The B-18Bs were equipped with a special radar that would allow the plane to more easily scan the surface for submarines, magnetic anomaly detection equipment (again, to help detect submarines), and a change in depth charge location (FRA 1988, 188). Normally depth charges were loaded in the fuselage bomb bay, but tests and limited operations were carried out fitting the depth charges beneath the wings which fired the bombs in a backward pattern. By August of 1943, the B-18Bs were replaced with the B-24s which could stay aloft for longer periods of time and most B-18Bs were used as cargo planes or crop sprayers (FRA 1988, 192).

They were using their special equipment, so it was interesting to listen in on the plane's interphone to the conversation between pilot, radio operator, and bombardier. We saw a lot of our freighters in convoys. I kind of wondered if any of the patrol boats were Gordon's. When you sit up there right behind the pilot watching what he has to check on takeoff and landing, it looks like quite a job. The pilot uses a typewritten check list to make sure he forgets nothing. Once in the air there is quite a bit of talk over the interphone each member of the crew having a headset and a small microphone. Part of it is routine checks and reports, part of it kidding each other.

I want to get this in the mail so I won't put in our system of location. I will try it some other time.

You have been wonderful about letters pleasing me no end. I walk up to the orderly tent when the mail has come in half hoping there will a letter with your neat little hand on it, but just knowing that it would be foolish to expect another so soon, but sure enough there it is, and I am very pleased.

I would love to see Georgia in that blue dress. She must be a picture.

My best to Rob when you see him.

Much love
George

[To George]
[Handwritten, possibly on 9/11/42]
[Locations unknown]

Darling,

The party was a huge success. Robbie couldn't come which was the only disappointment. In the end I had 14. Tom Turbell couldn't get there the last minute but Pete Peters and Peggy Jerli joined us after we got to the club. I was covered with flowers. Chloe sent me an orchid and George Hite sent both Chloe and me 3 gardenias. I managed to get into that red dinner dress of mine—the one with the jersey top and chiffon skirt. The jersey part stretches so it just let me in and it really looked very well considering. I didn't take anything to drink but a small sherry which kept me feeling O.K. We all had cocktails before dinner and a nice dinner. I let them buy their own drinks. I didn't know what to do about tipping so I just gave $5.00 to Tommy (head waiter) and asked him to take care of it. I left before the party broke up as "whatchamacallit" seems to like his sleep. Pete P. insisted on following me home which seemed silly. I outgrew that months ago. It was nice of him, though. I felt pretty good when I drove in the garage and before I could get the lights

off Doxie was there wagging his tail and welcoming me—
ready to escort me safely to the door. Even Pete noticed it. He
said, "you really do have a gentleman living with you, after
all."

The best thing about the party was that yesterday Pete
Bauscaren received a marvelous offer from Macy's and
they aren't leaving Greenwich after all. Chloe was terribly
embarrassed, but I thought that gave all the more reason for
the party. She says she's going to give me a "coming out
party." As each and every one said goodnight to me they
asked about you and wanted their thanks extended and
expressed the desire to have you here very soon.

I must get up and go to the village. There's a Dr's
appointment at 10.00 and a million and one errands to be
done. I'm enclosing a letter from Aunt Mary to Mother
which was forwarded to me. It's rather encouraging about
Ford. I don't know if it means he's all right now or not but
it's something.

Here's Larry he has a message for you. I asked him
what he said. It's "Dear Daddy."

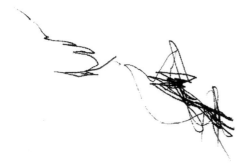

You should have heard the song he was singing [to] me from his bed this morning. He woke me up announcing that he was about to sing me a song about a horsey. It went "Horsey, horsey-----jibber and nonsense---horsey don't go big toidey in the road----more jibber and nonsense---- Momie will spank you----etc." I didn't dare pretend I heard it.

All my love
Peggy

[To George]
[Handwritten, probably on 9/12/42]
[Locations unknown]

My darling:

Here's another rainy day. I expect to spend most of it knitting and sewing for the children. I nearly have their winter clothes all ready and haven't spent $5.00 on them except for shoes. I interlined an old pink spring coat of Larry's for Georgia and with a sweater beneath, she can wear it for dress all winter. I'm knitting her a pair of white leggings to go with it. You saw the green pants I knit Larry and I have the blue ones here nearly done. I've also made him two yellow cotton shirts to go with them and knitted caps to match. On my sewing machine I've finished two pairs of flannel pajamas for him with feet even. It helps to keep busy and is rather fun too.

Robbie phoned again last night. He was just leaving to go back to camp. Said his Father would be in Mlps on Tues: so I wrote a note to Daddy in hopes he can see him.

In the end I took Tina and both children to Greenwich after I wrote you yesterday. I finally got Georgia's hair cut which almost broke my heart. She doesn't look nearly as cute but they say it's the only way it will ever thicken up and she has two spots almost bald. Larry got his winter shoes and we did a million errands. The Doctor said I'm fine. My weight is "remarkable" says he, but you should see me. He discovered the baby is what they call a "breach." It means coming feet first. I've had a feeling it was for some time. He said he thought he could turn it around and I'll be darned if he didn't. It was the craziest feeling. By just manipulating my tummy he turned it completely around. You could see it turn as plain as could be. It didn't hurt a bit.

Larry's arrived and wants me to play "Pacino's" records for him. It's just the kind of day for it so I guess I'll get up and fix his phonograph.

I had a wonderful letter from you yesterday. It's so nice to know somebody's down there for you to talk to. I'm not surprised the Colonel and Majors were impressed with the service you gave them. They should be. For a second I was paralyzed when you said you'd write in a location by our prearranged method next time. Gosh! Am I going to be a sissy if you really go! I still don't believe you will. You're too important here.

At 6:30 this morning Doxie and I were out in the yard keeping the cows at bay until help arrived. They've been out in this field nearly a week and I've expected a call every day. It was a little surprising to be awakened by a great "moo oo" right under my window. Doxie nearly jumped out of his skin, but then got real brave.

I don't expect you to write me as often as I'm doing now, so don't even attempt it. As for your pictures, Betty Hite is going to do them this next week. Sorry to keep you waiting but she's busy as Junior League Pres. with something they are doing Sat.

Must be going again.

All yours always
Peggy

[To Peggy]
[Handwritten, probably on 9/13/42, postmarked 9/13/42 at 6 PM[70]]
[From Key West, FL to Greenwich, CT]

My darling,

There is some good news so I will save it for the very last part of this letter, don't look now.

Played golf this morning not too badly, but the mosquitoes were terrible. They have been driving us crazy here for the last few days. We have had some heavy rains I guess that is the cause.

The company has not been bad here since these alert crews have been kept down here. Most of the officers are between twenty-four and thirty. There don't seem to be many of them from the north, so I hear a lot of that friendly Dixie drawl.

Last night I ate one dinner then when some of the officers came in from a late patrol I took them down to get some dinner and had some more myself.

---

[70] Sunday postmarks appear sporadically throughout the collection although the mail was not processed on Sundays.

I will write Baxter[71] about you coming out to Minneapolis. I am going to send him a box of those five cent cigars they make down here, might break him of chewing tobacco.

Oh I can hardly wait until I get to the end of this letter to tell you the real news. Well, just so you will not leave for the West before I get there, here it is.

I had a note from Major Clatanoff[72] saying that First Air Force had ordered an Air Base Group up in Miami to replace us down here as soon as possible, so I would guess that we will be starting back in a week or ten days.

Be glad to see me? Tell Larry and Georgia that maybe daddy is coming home.

Yours with love, George.

---

[71] Baxter was a male nanny for George and Ki when they were growing up.

[72] Possibly Lt. Colonel Walter George William Clatanoff of the Army Air Corps.

[To George]
[Handwritten, probably on 9/15/42]
[Locations unknown]

My Darling,

It's seems days since I've written you. It's gotten to be fun talking to you every morning before I get up so that I miss it when I skip a day. Sunday I cannot write as the mail doesn't go out and yesterday I had to dash in to N.Y.C. early.

Saturday I didn't do a thing but be domestic and knit and play with the children. It rained most all day. That evening with Tina's help I made another colored title for our movies of the children. All through the job I kept thinking of the night I made the other one in Forest Hills and you came home from your class and were so excited to see what I'd been doing. It was sort of like playing house in those days wasn't it? We'll do it again too. This title we did all with dolls for Georgia and one floppy eared dog who raised his ears very quizzically over the words "Baby Georgia."

I was thrilled over the pictures I'm enclosing. The one of you and Larry I have right by my bed. Doesn't he look tall? The other of Georgia is of course your darling little daughter on her second birthday. Don't you love it? I think you can figure out the children around the tree.

Sunday was a beautiful day. I spent it entirely outdoors in the blue chair watching the children play. What a perfect spot this yard is for their romping. They play follow-the-leader, turning millions of somersaults and riding the horsey (big rock by the play pen), running around on the bench under the apple tree etc., etc. After their naps I took them up to Hekma's for a party for Bryce. They had sailboats in their little pool on the lawn and Larry had the time of his life. I left them in Tina's care and came home. Mr. Ryan drove the horses and a wagon full of hay up there and took them all for a hay ride. I wish I'd seen them. They came home just pop-eyed. Larry was still talking about it long after he went to bed. Georgia, it seems, insisted on holding on to the reigns and telling the horses "hurry-up cows." All animals except Doxie are cows. Sunday night I went to a lovely party at the Terbells. According to Bernice's standard, we have now arrived in Greenwich society. They really are two swell people. It was a beautiful buffet supper—about like one Jessie would put on—elaborate, and delicious. Then I played bridge with Tom Terbell against Chloe and George Hite. We won $4.60. My luck has changed, perhaps. There was also a very stiff poker game which was too big for my pleasure. You can imagine the stakes. Jeane Beane won $24.00 in 2 hours.

Yesterday Betty Hite and I made a trip to N.Y.C. and had a real spree. Gimel's had a sale of real imported silks— about the last we'll see for some years and I bought 5. Two for dinner dresses and 3 summer prints. When this is over I'll have them made up for you and we'll have that second honeymoon. I also bought us a few Christmas cards (only 50) of a[n] 1890 Country village scene. Then I got 25 real cute ones for the children to send of a little dutch brother and sister looking out of the bed clothes in their little dutch bed on a tiny Christmas tree and presents. We had lunch at Tony's Trouville and I took two last winter hats to be fixed up. Then I tried to get you another penknife, but they only have domestic ones left. I didn't get one, but easily can if you want it. Let me know. Otherwise I can send the Swiss one the Clows gave you.

Have you ever heard from Gilly? I'm wondering if his boat ever got in. Also, what about the Streets?

Your description of going up on patrol was fascinating. That must be a really thrilling experience to see the convoys at night and listen in on the plane phones.

Well here I am at the bottom [of the page]. It's another nice day. Poor little Georgia has a cold, so Larry and Doxie and I will have to go out alone.

All our love

Peggy

[To George]
[Handwritten, possibly on 9/16/42]
[Locations unknown]

Darling,

This is a very foggy morning. I am supposed to be playing golf with Helen Gorton in an hour and a half. It will probably clear up by then.

The blue chair had me all day yesterday. It became very hot in the afternoon, and I came in for a while for a nap. Georgia was in bed all day with her cold except for an hour outdoors in the sun. She seems much better today.

Last night I went to Martha Buckhaut's for dinner. Clay was at a convention so she had 4 girls for dinner and bridge. One was Mary Dudley Gillespie whose husband left on the clipper two weeks ago for New Delhi, India with the Donovan Com. The other is Ann Hanan. Her husband called 'Moon' Hanan was in the legal dept. of Union Carbon and Carbide with Robbie.[73] He now is at sea on a "Corvette" as Executive Officer. She doesn't expect to see him until the war is over. She's looking for a house, incidentally,

---

[73] Robin Peake worked as a lawyer with the Union Carbide Carbon Corp.

Oct. 1. And I offered her this until Jan. She's coming Mon. night for dinner to talk it over. It'll work if she can get help. At present she's alone with an 11 month old baby & expects another in April. We had a very interesting evening. It was a treat to see people who do a little thinking on their own. It seems as if the only girls who think about the world situation at all are those whose personal lives are so disrupted by this war. Otherwise, they go blissfully on as usual thinking only of children and the day's marketing problems.

Larry is sitting on my bed putting his shoes and stockings on and jabbering like a magpie until I don't know what I'm saying. Right here he caught his foot in the telephone cord and sent the phone piece flying under your bed.

I'll have to cut this short to get my work done if I'm playing golf.

All my love
Peggy

P.S. Have you figured out if it pays for me to put on Air Mail or not.

[To George]
[Handwritten, possibly on 9/17/42]
[Locations unknown]

Darling,

Well maybe this household isn't all in a tizzy over your arrival. We can hardly stand it with all the excitement. Larry and I are already competing over what's to be done with every second you are home. If you or Georgia have any ideas, you better forget them right now. You should have seen me trying to wait until the end of your letter to find out what was up. I thought I read each word in order but when I finished and then reread it I knew I'd retained nothing at first but the last paragraph.

I have Larry in bed today with the cold. He was miserable all night. He's in my bed making sailboats on a magazine and sniffling. I'm sitting here on the chaise keeping him company. We're both waiting for breakfast. Georgia seems to feel better today. Hodgie was supposed to come up and play today. I'll have to call it off.

My golf yesterday was good. I had a 51 which is as good as I've ever done on the first 9. Nine holes is about all

I can take now. Maybe I'll have to stay pregnant to play well. I must say the swing is rather impeded. Helen and I had lunch at the club and then I got my errands done in town.

I went to Marjorie's for dinner as Pete was in town. We talked a while after dinner and I was home by 10.00. She had another butler last night. Since I saw you there's also been a nurse come and go. I should think she'd keep one just because she'd get so tired of breaking them in every week or so.

Now I've finished breakfast and Larry is eating off his tray, jabbering away. He's arrived at the questioning stage and there's nothing to do but answer him truthfully and to his complete understanding and satisfaction. Otherwise he'll repeat and repeat until Kingdom come.

Larry just came out with "Momie, Daddy's watching me eating. He says 'you're a good boy Larry to eat like that. I'm coming to see you soon." It started from seeing your picture on my dresser. He's so proud of being in a picture with you, he mentions it every time he comes into the room. He says, "See me with my Daddy. He's holding my hand and smiling at my Momie."

Well, of all things Hodgie just arrived. Pete left him before I had a chance to phone and was gone before I got downstairs. Now Hodgie is here on the floor playing with Larry's boats and they are giggling back and forth. He'll probably go home with a cold. Marjorie didn't have anyone to leave him with today, but I hardly expected him at 8:30. I suppose I'd better take him outdoors and amuse him away from Larry.

You've no doubt read of our awful Kidnapping in Bedford.[4] Two little girls 7 & 8 sisters were taken Sunday night and found raped (if you can imagine anything as horrible) beaten, and killed in Beaver Dam Brook night before last. That little brook runs right through the village under the main road after you turn right by that row of

---

[74] On Monday evening, September 14, 1942, Helen and Margaret Lynch, ages 8 and 7 respectively, were kidnapped while walking home. The 17-year-old who kidnapped them had stolen a car and attempted to kidnap a couple of other women before he picked up the two young girls. The teenager bound and gagged them, assaulted them, then mutilated their bodies with a knife. Margaret was tossed out of the moving car then retrieved and thrown into a brook near Bedford where she drowned and was found the next day by playmates of hers walking by to take a swim. Helen was placed in the road and the kidnapper drove the car back and forth over her until she was dead. Her remains were left in the Kensico Reservoir. They were found after the kidnapper confessed to the crimes and led police to the spot where he had discarded Helen's body (NYT 09/16/1942, 19). The kidnapper was eventually caught, charged, and despite attempts to prove he was insane, found guilty. At the time of his execution, he was the youngest criminal in the state of New York to die in the electric chair (NYT 07/09/1943, 19).

pretty old houses. Thank God, they've already caught the maniac.

I just got the morning paper and a 3 year old has been kidnapped in Pelham.[75] Again they've caught the kidnapper. I guess there are things pretty horrible _besides_ war.

My boys are getting pretty noisy. Guess I'll have to separate them.

Again, I can't tell you how happy you've made us all. When are you leaving.

All love
Peggy

---

[75] On Friday September 18, 1942 in Pelham, New York, a nursemaid allegedly was kidnapped along with her four-year-old charge. They were held for a $30,000 ransom for 12 hours and then released when the ransom was not paid. The FBI alleges the kidnapping was a hoax, elaborated by the nursemaid in order to extort her employers (NCN 09/18/1942).

[To George]
[Handwritten, probably later the same day as above or 9/17/42]
[Locations unknown]

Dearest George,

This is just a short note to say both children are better this morning and we have hopes of being out tomorrow. I still haven't gotten the cold and am doing everything to prevent it.

Larry and I are both in bed in the guest room this morning. He was awfully miserable late yesterday with a temperature and up most the night. After aspirin and an enema about 5:30 this morning his temp. is down and he's eating a good breakfast now.

I sort of hope you may have left before this reaches you, but until I know when you are going for sure I'll keep writing.

Marjorie came for Hodgie finally about 4:30. We certainly were busy keeping the boys apart and watching all three. Your darling efficient wife is certainly a sucker to say the least.

I forgot to tell you I entered some of my jelly and canned stuff in the flower show (Greenwich) yesterday and they phoned me to say I won 1st prize with my jelly. Ain't that something? It's a nasty day today but I'm going to have to go over and see the show now.

Tonight I'm going to Helen Groton's for a girl's dinner and bridge game.

All my love
Peggy

[To George]
[Handwritten, possibly on 9/19/42[76]]
[Locations unknown]

Darling

Larry is much better. He's driving me crazy in fact. I'm lying in a bed of toys including, puzzles, games, boats, airplanes, shovels and books. It's raining again today so I'm going to keep them in another day. They both have coughs still anyway. Walt Disney's movie of the baby deer "Bambi" is in Greenwich. This is the last day and I had hoped to take Larry. He knows the book and loves the story.

I had a nice letter from Mom yesterday. She certainly is looking forward to getting us out there. It will do them both good. She forwarded a letter from Dexter to Dad which I'll send on with this. He seems to be pretty well in the midst of things.

I went to the Woman's Exchange for lunch yesterday with Jeane, Helen Gorton, Chloe, Sue Sutter, Betty Hite and Marj. Adams. Then we all went to the Y.M.C.A to the flower show. I wish you could have seen my jelly with the big blue seal on it. I had 11 competitors too so I felt

---

[76] The day of the flower show was the previous day, as mentioned in the "Friday" letter.

really good. My raspberry jam got honorable mention. As soon as you arrive I'll give you some for breakfast.

My hours seem to be spent now wondering what day you'll be leaving and how quickly after that I can begin looking for you. It's going to be such fun. Have you put in for leave? Better do it and we'll worry about Christmas later. If you could get a week now and another then, it would be perfect. But that's too much to hope for with the luck we've had so far in that line.

Last night Helen Gorton had a hen party with Ann Hanan, Mary Gillespie again and Alice Sturgis. We were going to have a cut in bridge game, but a discussion started on Washington versus the war effort which lasted until 11:30 when we all went home.

Georgia just climbed on the bed to attack me and the toys. What a shambles. She walked straight over my stomach upsetting a box of colored paper pieces (at least 500 in all). Here comes Larry too so I might as well give up and get up. All send love and can hardly wait to see you.

Peggy

[To George]
[Handwritten, possibly on 9/20/42[77]]
[Locations unknown]

I stopped at Twyeffort's last week and got these samples of material. His price for blouse and pants is only $140.00. Let me know if you want them.

Darling,

You've been so good about writing this week. I'm afraid you are going to spoil me. I found yesterday's letter waiting when I returned from a golf game with Jeane and Helen Gorton. Had I known it was here I never could have stayed over all day. When the money dropped out I could hardly believe my eyes. It's a wonderful idea and I'm going to add a bill to every one you send if they aren't all that size. That was just a good big one to start with, I imagine. Won't we have fun on that trip? This makes it all seem closer too when we save the actual funds to go on. (Is it safe to mail the bills?)

---

[77] This letter is placed here because Peggy's commitments could not have been completed as she says if they had taken place on any other weekend. The activities of her other weekends are accounted for in dated letters.

Thursday and Friday this week I spent sewing at the Red Cross. I had intended to only stay at the church Thurs. morning and then two others and myself were all out of 10 who showed up and we had 50 service bags to make. I wish I could have swiped one for you. They are about 15 inches square and are for your toilet articles. Anyhow out of 3 of us only two knew how to use a machine so I peddled a foot sewing machine until 5:30 and we finished them. Then of course our regular sewing was way behind as we had to drop everything to do the bags so I brought 6 baby sacks home and used my own machine all day Friday making those. There certainly was some difference in the work mine turned out and the little effort it required.

Thurs. P.M. Alice Sturgis (her husband is stationed in Congress Hotel, Chicago—Air Corps training center) and I went to Beanes for dinner. We played bridge afterwards and had a very nice evening. Yesterday—Sat. after golf, Jeane and I took a swim and sat around the pool most of the afternoon. I ran into the Hites and Bowdens who were unoccupied for the evening and got them to come over for supper. Berenice brought some corn she had and I happened to have 5 molds of salmon gelatin salad, cucumber, and <u>our</u>

own tomatoes. Then I made a blueberry shortcake out of a can of blueberries from the Manchester Commissary. George Hite was bartender and we ate on the porch, and all wished you were here. Had a little game of poker afterwards at which I lost $1.00. I haven't held bridge or poker hands for 3 months now. Must be true about "Unlucky at cards, lucky in love." I know the latter part is true more every day of my life. How I should get such a marvelous man is more of a mystery to me every day. You haven't a prayer of ever getting away from me either.

Daddy sent me a copy of the letter he wrote you.[78] He seemed very pleased over the presents you've sent. I also was interested in his comments on M.-Moline. He amused me too with Thelma and my "waist to waist" race.

When I returned from Key West there was a nice letter here from Nell Clow. I'll try to find it and enclose it.

Today was pretty hot. I went to Bill and Bernice's for a cocktail at noon to meet some new neighbors. Then we all joined the Hites at the Club for dinner around 3. Now it's 6:30 and I should be at a cocktail party at Mussey's but

[78] This letter, with the note to Peggy, is included in Additional Letters.

I'm in my nightie instead sitting on the porch writing you and enjoying a beautiful bowl of flowers from our garden. Mussey arrived back this week after moving her child and furniture to a rented apt. in N.J. and then breaking the lease and returning all since I left for Key West. She's being sued for breaking the lease, has no help and very little money. She must be crazy!!

Incidentally the fuel oil situation looks so bad for this locality this winter that I'm thinking of approaching Hekma now to convert this to coal. What do you think? I'd hate to get back Jan. 1st with a new baby and insufficient heat. Also hate to shovel coal.

The children are fine, I'm fine, Doxie's fine and we all love you very much and miss you more than words can ever say. Yours always.

Peggy

[To Peggy]
[Handwritten, probably 9/26/42, postmarked on 9/28/42 at 11:30 AM]
[From Key West, FL to Greenwich, CT]

Peggy dear,

You must be getting ever so tired of being told how much I love you, but I do so very much. ⌉⌈ *Sunday* Now that is all the further I got last night when I was rudely interrupted by Capt. Cole and another officer.

They just wanted to talk so we smoked and discussed our Air Force how we thought it could be improved and then what we thought the world would be like after the war. Cole is very interested in South America and wants to operate an airline in Brazil after the war.

I have made some good friends among the officers who come down here. They stay here two or three days at a time two crews at a time, but I see them often as there are only 7 or 8 crews taking turns at coming down. They are a swell bunch of boys. Norton is down today, the boy I mentioned before from West Point. I have a bet with myself that he is going to be one of the top men in our air force some day. His navigator Lt. Jennings is another one I like to see come in. He plays a swell game of chess, so we have played a lot with me catching on so it isn't too easy for him now to win although he still does. Black Jack is the favorite card game by a long ways, and there is nearly always a game in progress.

I don't remember if I told you a couple of Sundays ago about going over to look through a submarine with a Lt. Smith a pleasant red headed fellow. Well a week ago Thursday he was landing here at night with Weiss and Green, two other officers, when they ran off the side of the runway just after landing completely washing out a B-18 and a night's sleep for me, but no one hurt.[79]

This last Thursday the same crew were cleared for a takeoff at 2 AM up at Miami. The B-18 they were in had just gotten up flying speed, loaded with 1,500 lbs of depth charges and 800 gallons of high octane gasoline when they ran head on into a big Army transport plane which was taxing up the runway to take off. The

---

[79] This accident is listed in the U.S. Army Air Force Accident reports for September 1942 as an LACNU or Landing Accident Nose Up. This type of accident usually happens when a pilot is attempting to land too near the runway threshold. The accident is listed as taking place on Tuesday, September 15 (AAIR 2009).

control operator had made a mistake. Norton just told me that when the fire was extinguished the next day nothing was left but a big puddle of melted metal.[80] When five, decent young men like that are taking these risks, while a bunch of loud mouth, labor agitators are holding up the war effort with selfish jurisdictional strikes to consolidate their ill gotten revenues they should be treated no different than traitors and saboteurs.

It is not only that these young men are fighting the war, they seem to be the ones who are most interested in planning and building a fine, fair, decent world to live in with their families when the war is over.

Friday I had a lot of fun taking one of the other officers over to the cigar factory, where he wanted to get some cigars for himself and his father. I sent George some real good cigars, thought it would be

---

[80] Just before dawn on Tuesday, September 22, 1942, this accident between a B-18 bomber and a transport craft on the runway happened as George describes. The officers who perished were First Lt. Charles M. Green, the 24-year-old pilot, 2nd Lt. Newell B. Smith Jr, the 21-year-old copilot, and Sergeant Walter Boehm, 30 years old. Injured were 22-year-old 2nd Lt. Lester Weiss, Sergeant G.H. Isenberg, and 22-year-old Private Wesley Johnson. George, at 29, was older than the majority of men involved in the crash. On board the transport craft, pilot Donald B. Johnson and co-pilot William F. Fortner were killed and their radio operator was severely burned (TMN 09/23/1942).

the last chance. Also I sent two boxes to Greenwich. They are very excellent cigars which might come in handy when you entertain or can be used for Christmas presents.

I think I will leave Miami Tuesday morning, but I will wire you when I know for sure. I have gotten everything turned over to the new outfit so I have not had much to do the last two days. Played golf today and took a swim. The outfit which is taking over are practically all recruits, but we have been working with them showing [them] the ropes, so I hope they make out well.

I would bet you would have gotten a laugh out of me doing a big wash and ironing job Friday. The men wanted to take a picture of me with the iron and send it to you. The work came out fine though.

Frank writes that he and Helen[81] will be in New York this week.

I am sorry to have upset your plans so about using the house. We will talk that over when I get to Greenwich which will be soon.

---

[81] Frank Steiner is George's first cousin. Helen is Frank's wife. George's father (Frank) named George after his brother (George), and George (the brother) named his son Frank after George's father.

I miss you so much my dear, and am very anxious to see you.

> With my love
> George (over)

[on the back]

I just have to tell you once more that I think you are the most wonderful girl in the world and love you so very, very much. I kind of like to tell you that, especially when you are in my arms.

[To George]
[Handwritten, possibly 10/4/42, postmarked 10/5/42 at 12:30 PM]
[From Greenwich, CT to Manchester, NH]

Darling!

Just a note before I go to bed. I've been sitting by the gratefire with Doxie just as we did last night, but with a completely different outlook. I've read the paper, knitted, played the Victrola, but all to no avail. Why are you such a necessity?

Our trip home last night was uneventful. After your departure even Doxie lost interest and put his head in my lap and slept all the way. This morning I wrote checks and letters.

About noon Anna asked for the afternoon and evening off which precipitated the storm I predicted to you yesterday. She had to cry which always makes me madder but in the end I think the tussle did us both good. I won out on the arguments and got my grievances aired and she got the evening off and $5.00 raise and is pretty much ashamed of herself, I hope.

I took Alice Sturges to the club for lunch and we

watched a bit of the tennis tournament. Everyone wanted to know why I hadn't brought you over even for 10 minutes last night. I, frankly, said "I wanted him all to myself." As a result I had to ask several to come next Sat. night before really knowing if you can make it.

Mother just phoned to ask about your visit. She couldn't believe we'd only had eight hours together. She sounded a bit more resigned to our not coming home so long as you may be around some time.

Now I'm going to bed and count off night #2 before I see you again. Larry was certainly disappointed when he crashed our door at 6:00 a.m squealing "Daddy" "Daddy can I get in your bed?" and found you gone. I had about 50 questions to answer and then he wasn't satisfied.

All yours 'til Friday—you better come
Peggy

[To Peggy]
[Handwritten[82] on 10/26/42, postmarked on 10/26/42 at 10:30 PM]
[From New York, NY to Greenwich, CT]

Darling:

Just thought I might just as well tell you that I love you, so long as I have to address an envelope anyway. Wish you were in here with me tonight. A hotel is kind of a lonely place. Guess I will never want to be a traveling salesman, it would be too lonely.

Give Larry and Georgia a kiss from Daddy. That number was Hempstead 821. It is the Headquarters of the First Air Service Area Command. (IASAC)

Love, George

---

[82] The first page of George's letter on Hotel Pennsylvania stationery is included in Memories.

[To Peggy]
[Handwritten,[83] possibly on 11/30/42]
[Locations unknown]

Dearest,

Here it is Monday morning, the first week and eight more to go.[84] They really keep us busy. Four hours of conferences in the morning, four in the afternoon plus another hour of optional instruction which is one of those affairs that everyone finds expedient to attend. Then you are encouraged not to study after eleven. Breakfast is 630 class at 800 so with 30 minutes for walking to breakfast and to class 20 minutes for breakfast I still have about 40 minutes left all to myself in which I can write you.[85] So that will give you a pretty good idea of what I do all day.

---

[83] The first page of George's letter on Fort Leavenworth stationery is included in Memories.

[84] Most classes were 9 weeks until they were changed to 10 weeks (TYL 1951, 11).

[85] Fort Leavenworth rose to the challenge of its mission—to produce large numbers of trained staff officers quickly—and did so with great success. The attendees were chosen from all over the Armed Forces based on their records and recommendations and were sent all over the world upon graduation. By late August 1944, 8,359 post Pearl Harbor graduates had been trained at Fort Leavenworth (TYL 1951, 22). George's descriptions of his classes and their activities are identical to the details provided in Tyler's official report (TYL 1951, 13-15).

The work is interesting; situations laid out on maps then we have to figure out what to do about it and the whole thing is very much in dead earnest as about half of the instructors and many of the students are just back from fights all over the world. It is queer to hear them tell about their experiences, usually not in a bragging way, just quiet almost emotionless about being in a fox hole all night with shells breaking all around or seeing German machine gunners in tanks refuse to fire on the crews, of disabled Allied tanks, who were walking back.[86] *Well I have to go now, it was swell to talk to you yesterday.*

All my love
George

---

[86] It is possible instructors and/or students at Fort Leavenworth were in Europe to witness the famous halting of German tanks at Dunkirk in late May and early June 1940 as Allied troops retreated. It is the most well-known example where German machine gunners in tanks were forced to watch the Allied troops retreating without being able to fire. Officially, however, there were only British, Belgian, and French troops fighting at that time but Americans served as volunteer fighters in the Canadian Armed Forces and the British Royal Air Force well before the U.S. entered the war. The Command and General Staff School at Fort Leavenworth frequently employed wounded WWII veterans as instructors when there were not enough regular Army officers necessary for faculty (SCH 2010, 162). It is also worth noting that in 1942, teams of Fort Leavenworth instructors travelled to each active theater to visit with commanders, staff officers, and course graduates to better determine what changes were needed at Fort Leavenworth to help ready soldiers for this modern battlefield (SCH 2010, 163). It is possible they are relating stories they heard and did not experience firsthand.

[To Peggy]
[Handwritten, possibly on 12/1/42, postmarked 11/31/42[87] at 11 AM]
[From Fort Leavenworth, KS to New York Hospital, New York, NY]

Peggy dear,

It was quite a trip out here. The plane did not leave N.Y. until 11 P.M. I started to phone you about 10 o'clock remembering you said you were going to listen for the plane, but thought you might have fallen asleep. I got talking to another officer who was coming out here to school a Capt. Carly and to another young fellow about my age who is building ships and so traveling under gov't priority. His name was MacFarlane and he had lived in Mpls, but no relation to our friends.

We got as far as Pittsburgh, where the T.W.A. took us downtown getting us some rooms for the night in a hotel. Next morning there was more confusion, but MacFarlane and I caught a train for Kansas City via Columbus, and St. Louis scheduled for 26 hours travel and the transfers with nothing but coaches. Carly got lost in the shuffle in Pittsburgh and is not here yet. Last I saw of him he was getting in a cab with a marine and an old lady to try to

---

[87] The envelope front, along with the unusual postmark, can be seen in Memories.

catch the train we took.

The train was packed, people sitting on luggage in the aisles of old rickety coaches while soldiers drained whiskey bottles and children ate bananas and oranges. We stopped at every crossroad. MacFarlane was a good fellow so we passed time talking. They did hitch on a diner and we ate with a retired naval officer who was a good gent. He had been in Johnny Bargesses classes at Annapolis and having been injured is on a retired list.

In the afternoon we got to Columbus Ohio where we were to transfer. Seats were scarce so we gave our bags to a red cap. MacFarlane ran over and got us a couple of seats on the coach and I ran upstairs to a phone [and] called the airport to see if there was any hope. The weather was beginning to clear a little so they said they would send a car in for us and that there probably would be a plane for Kansas City. After some trouble getting our luggage off the train before it pulled out, and an argument with a T.W.A. over tickets which the T.W.A. in Pittsburgh had exchanged for rail tickets we took off landing in Kansas City at 9 P.M. Sunday night.

I caught a bus which got me out here at 1145 P.M. Sunday night. It just went to a reception center for drafters at a far corner of the port. After some phone calls I got a recon to pick me up, signed in at Hdq, got my room and went to bed.

I won't go into any more details, but I did arrive at the proper class, seated in the proper seat, appear presentable, all necessary papers filled out, having obtained all my text books which would not begin to go into my brief case, had read the first assignment, and had breakfast, all by 8 o'clock. [88]

I will write you about Ft Leavenworth and the School next time. Looks like it is going to be a lot of work.

Your letter just arrived thanks so much. Glad to hear you and Robbie[89] are getting acquainted. We sure have a dandy family now Larry, Georgia, and Robbie sounds good. R.R. Steiner that will make a good signature.

I love you very much dear,
George

---

[88] Colonel Tyler, in his report on the history of Fort Leavenworth makes it clear that, "everything was done for the student...he was made to feel that the Post and school existed only to facilitate his primary mission; that is his graduation as a trained staff officer" (13). George's descriptions of his quarters, his courses, even the orderly and his service, align perfectly with the example routine detailed in the history writeup (13-15).

[89] Robin R. Steiner was born on November 26, 1942.

[To Peggy]
[Handwritten, probably on 12/4/42, postmarked 12/4/42]
[From Fort Leavenworth, KS to New York Hospital, New York, NY]

Darling:

Last night before going to sleep I was lying in bed think[ing] what a swell family we have. It seems hard to believe that little Robbie is really with us now. I can't wait to get my hands on him and begin to get acquainted. With us three men in the family now, we ought to be able to take good care of our two women.

Well I suppose you would like to hear about this place. The post of Ft. Leavenworth sits on a high bluff to the West of the Missouri river. It is an old fort with well built old red brick buildings well spaced along wide streets with a number of open grass squares. The roads are lined with big old elm trees. The school buildings sit on the top of the bluff overlooking the Missouri, with the other buildings lined along streets which slant quite steeply in places down the bluff away from the river. There are the usual cavalry barracks with some fairly decent looking horses.

It is still pitch dark out, but I have shaved, dressed, had

breakfast with a cold ten minute walk each way, studied a map assignment and said hello to you. Now I have to start for class and mail this on the way over. They keep us really busy.

Thanks for your very good letters, 3 of them already. My address is apt. 1, 320 Donipshan Place, Ft Leavenworth, Kansas.

I love you so very much and miss you dear.

My love
George

[To Peggy]
[Handwritten, [90] probably on 12/6/42, postmarked on 12/10/42]
[From Fort Leavenworth, KS to New York Hospital, New York, NY[91]]

My darling Peggy,

Your voice sounded so good today. I think you must have been very pleased to have Irene and George there with you today. I certainly wish that I could have been part of that party. Are they duly impressed with Robbie and Miss Georgia and Master Larry. I tell you I feel mighty proud every time I think of them which is often.

I have a little picture here on the desk of Georgia sitting on your lap out on the lawn this summer. You are a couple of pretty nice looking girls. Then there is one of Larry swinging Georgia which would really bear enlarging.

I got a couple of other officers to walk down to the town of Leavenworth for dinner today. It is about an hour's walk and sure was cold. But it was good to get away from here and we got a good

---

[90] The first page of George's letter on Fort Leavenworth stationery is included in Memories.

[91] Peggy was most likely still in the hospital after Robin's birth.

steak dinner. This is a dry state, but a little persuasion got us a drink.[92] I hope you get a Christmas tree. It might be a good chance to get one while your father is there.

I got all my work for tomorrow finished yesterday so I have time today to write a number of letters, read the paper, and go to town. They throw it at us pretty fast during the week so it helps to get a break like that. I was going to go over to the movies, but decided to stay here and get off a couple of more letters.

The rooms are a bit bleak. This was a married officer's apartment before the war when the classes were small here. Now seven of us share the apartment. The walls are mostly lined with compoboard to fasten our maps to with lights riding along in front of them on pulleys. We each have a table, a chair and an iron bed, a bureau too. There are four bedrooms, two baths, a kitchen, a combination dining room living room, and a small room which opens off of the living toward the front. The other six boys have the four bedrooms and I have the front room which is the most pleasant as it

---

[92] Despite the 18th amendment being repealed in 1933, alcoholic liquor was not legalized in Kansas until 1948 (KHS 2001).

faces to the south out toward the golf course with a pleasant sunny prospect during the day. We have a colored orderly who is really good. Nothing to complain about, after Key West and Carolina it is palatial. All my love to the dearest girl in the world. I miss you so much.

George

[To George]
[Handwritten, probably on 12/6/42[93]]
[Locations unknown]

Darling;

It was wonderful to talk to you this morning. We've been wishing that you could be with us all day. The children have been in bed pretty much all day. Their colds are much better. We brought Larry down in front of the fire after his supper and we all looked at our movies of skiing, Williamsburg, and the children. You know how much that pleased him.

After the movies Mom, Dad & I went out in the kitchen and got supper of creamed pheasant, toast, milk, salad and cake. We ate on the card table here in front of the fire. I kept thinking how we'd done the same thing just a few weeks ago. We used the same cloth and napkins which I told you I'd made. Mother says I was 13 instead of 10 as I told you.

Now Mother and Dad are sitting here in the living room reading while I say hello to you. Mom just went up in

---

[93] George also mentions he and Peggy chatted on the phone in his Sunday letter from 12/6/42.

the attic with my flashlight and got your riding boots, skates etc. We'll get them off right away. The Holiday mail may delay things a bit.

Our snowfall never stopped until dark. It's perfectly lovely here. Too bad it couldn't have been Christmas today. The big pine tree was just covered with snow and the branches bent way low with the weight of it. Doxie was just foolish trying to be a puppy again rolling in it. He tried to coax someone to play in it. I know he thought "Oh, if George were only here."

I'm feeling stronger and looking better every day. My weight is back to normal but the waist line isn't. Robbie is fine again today. His tummy was upset for a couple of days. It was pathetic the way he'd eat avidly and then everything would come back (a little hard on our guest room rug. I must say!)

I'm enclosing this card from Ass. Hosp. Service for our address. It never occurred to me when I signed the receipt for their services that maybe I shouldn't have given the North St. address since the plant pays the insurance. Consequently, [I] think you'd better answer this so there will be no mix up.

As Christmas approaches I'm rapidly wishing it were over. If it weren't for the children I'd skip the whole thing gladly. I just can't imagine having any fun without you. Let's pray it will never happen again.

Guess I'll have to give Robbie his 10 P.M. feeding. So here's my love and I'll write again tomorrow.

Yours always.
Peggy

P.S. What's Matthews' address?

As I reread this I can see that the radio going ∧*in my ear* wreaked its usual havoc on my concentration. Please forgive.

[To George]
[Handwritten, probably 12/18/42[94]]
[Locations unknown]

Dearest George,

Mom and I have just finished our breakfasts here in bed. And is it cold here. We still have the snow and this morning there is more with the temperature below zero again. It was -10° yesterday. We are keeping fairly comfortable but I'm getting the cold today. Surely hope it's over for Christmas.

The morning paper just arrived and with less than a day's supply of gas on the east coast, they are cutting out all A cards. Thank goodness the cars are full, but what we'll do after that, I don't know, but I shall wait to worry about that. Probably with this cold spell, all tankers are directed to bringing fuel oil instead of gasoline.

Larry is thrilled this morning with Jack Frost's handiwork. We have regular fairy forests and animals on all the windows. Incidentally except for a bit of a cough now

---

[94] On December 18, 1942 the front page of the *New York Times* ran an article describing the imminent rationing of A-cards along the East Coast of the United States. This is most likely the article Peggy references in the letter (NYT 12/18/1942, 1).

and then from Georgia, the children are over their colds. They haven't been out of doors yet and won't until it's warmer now. As soon as I can go to N.Y. I'm going to take her (Georgia) to a skin specialist. She's had three more spots and they came from scratches. It looks to me now as if she has a skin condition which I can vaguely remember studying. It's just a rare type of skin which infects readily and scars wherever there is any break at all. I sincerely hope I'm wrong, cause I recall there's nothing to do for it. Larry scratched her on the neck 2 weeks ago and the nail marks all left scars and one became infected just like that on her forehead. Enough of our ailments!

Robbie is coming along fine. He sat in Larry's lap yesterday which seemed to delight them both. Larry looked him over from stem to stern asking all sorts of questions, "What do we have fingers for? What do we have necks for? What do we have eyes for?" I answered the first two and then told him to answer the last for himself. He said, "I have eyes to look with but Robbie has eyes to sleep with." When he'd held him long enough he handed him back and said, "Robbie needs to go toidey now."

Mother and I taught the girls backgammon last night.

It was interesting to watch the difference in their minds. After one game Tina had a pretty good idea of what it was all about, but after 6 games Anna was still pushing the men backwards. Nevertheless, she's a swell girl.

Mom sends her love and says not to worry she'll stick to us whether we try to starve or freeze her out. As a matter of fact she's a darn good sport about the cold. Coming from a house always evenly heated to 70° she notices this much more but I keep her in sweaters and she hasn't complained.

Anna's ready to go to town & take this so until tomorrow.

All yours
Peggy

1943

January –May

[To George]
[Handwritten, probably on 1/4/43, postmarked 1/6/43 at 11:30 AM]
[From Greenwich, CT to Fort Leavenworth, KS]

My darling,

So much will have happened by the time you receive this letter that it's almost foolish to try and write, but I am too worried to get busy at housework and it seems a comfort just to talk to you like this. Your letter written New Year's Eve and New Year's arrived this morning and I read it while walking along the snow on North St. to Congers for vegetables. It almost seems as if you were with me and I was so thrilled to know you love me as much this year as last.

I have just talked to Dr. Donovan over the phone and he says there is no need for any further observation. Robbie is slowly starving himself as his tummy holds virtually none of his feedings now. I have given written permission for him to operate tomorrow afternoon. It would be ridiculous to wait longer as the baby's chances of recovery diminish with his strength. When I sent you the telegram last night Dr. Donovan had given his opinion, from examination and use of Dr. Close's x-rays, as the worst of the three possibilities. Today he phoned and says he is certain that he will find pyloric stenosis[95] despite the existence of the X-rays showing constriction further down. He says he could feel the pyloric tumor "very satisfactorily" this morning. I asked him Robin's chances of recovery to which he replied "Of course any abdominal operation on an infant is serious, very serious; but your baby is in good condition still, despite continual vomiting and my guess is he'll come through clean as a wink." This operation was what we tried to avoid at first, but after the X-rays showed a possible small intestinal obstruction, we are relieved to only have the pyloric trouble. Robin has a private room and a fine night nurse who we talked to quite a while before coming home last night. Not going in today. I haven't met the day nurse. Mother is going in with me tomorrow to lend support through the operation. We'll stay at the Hospital tomorrow night. May God be with our little boy. He knows my voice now and looks so sick I can hardly look at him without crying. One comfort though is that Dr. Donovan said this is something he was born with, and I couldn't hold myself to blame in any way.

Anna and Tina are being wonderful. They keep me from

---

[95] Pyloric stenosis is a rare condition found in infants usually between three and five weeks after birth. The pylorus is a muscular valve that holds food in the stomach until the small intestine is ready for it in the next phase of digestion. Pyloric stenosis occurs when the pyloric muscles become too thick, blocking the food from entering the small intestine (MC 1998-2020).

the bother of answering the phone all day. I appreciate our friends calling, but there's nothing more to say now until the operation is over.

I'm enclosing a few notes which may interest you.

Please always know I've done the best I know how with Robbie and have made each decision asking myself "what would George say?"

Yours always Peggy

[on the back]

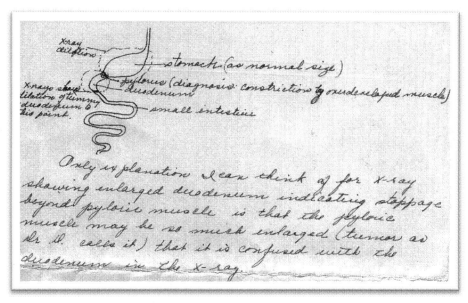

[from the above letter]

Only explanation I can think of for x-ray showing enlarged duodenum indicating stoppage beyond pyloric muscle is that the pyloric muscle may be so much enlarged (tumor as Dr. D. calls it) that it is confused with the duodenum in the x-ray.

[To Peggy]
[Handwritten, probably on 1/6/43, postmarked on 1/6/43 at 11 AM]
[From Fort Leavenworth, KS to Greenwich, CT]

My darling:

Here it is another morning with a cold wind howling around in the darkness outside, and ever since I first woke up with a longing to have you beside me, I have been thinking of you, how charming you look in a dinner gown, how beautiful you are in a nightie and without one too. You manage the house so well and take such good care of our children. In fact you are a perfect wife.

I got your telegram yesterday morning that the doctor was going to operate. All I could think about all day was poor little Robbie, how I wish I could do something for him. I was glad to get your telegram last night saying that he had come through all right. I am still praying for the little fellow. I don't suppose he is safe yet, I will certainly be glad to hear he is back home, but I would leave him in the hospital until you are very sure everything is all right.

I think it would be fine for you to go up to Lake Placid, but is not too long since you had Robbie so do be careful and don't try too much exercise.

Have to go now.

With so much love
George

[To George]
[Handwritten, probably on 1/6/43, postmarked 1/7/43 at 1:30 PM]
[From New York, NY to Fort Leavenworth, KS]

Darling,

Another crisis in our lives is behind us tonight and for the time being at least we still can look forward to having three lovely healthy children. What more could any two ask for?

Mother & I reached the hospital at noon yesterday and waited until five for him to go to the operating room. We sat in the waiting room most of the time because he cried almost continually by then and it was so pitiful to listen to. Miss O'Riley carried him upstairs at 5:00 and I thought I was going to weep when I saw the little fellow go out of his room. His eyes were wide open and he seemed to know something was happening which concerned him quite definitely. We waited what seemed an eternity (really not quite an hour) and he came back in Miss O'Riley's arms but looking quite differently of course. He was awfully white and breathed with difficulty and smelled of ether. She put him in bed and had his head much lowered with an oxygen tank right by the door until he came out of the anesthesia. He recovered unaided and has been gaining strength ever since. Tonight Miss Markuson said his temperature is nearly normal and he's taking about 20 cc of milk or water every 1 1/2 hours. His color is getting better and she claims he tried to talk to her and is sure he'll smile tomorrow. Both the nurses are <u>excellent</u>. They are special baby nurses about 35 yrs old and both are crazy about Robin. In fact all the nurses at Greenwich, as well, have said for a sick baby they never knew a tiny infant could be so good as he has all along. That's just like his Daddy.

Dr. Donovan is a marvelous man as well as surgeon. Mother & I liked him immediately. Miss O'Riley said he's noted all over the country for his infant surgery and he gets practically all the pyloric surgery in this part of the country. I'm so lucky to have called Dr. Wing about Robin before I let them go ahead out here. I don't think I would have any way, though. I must say Dr. Close did the diagnosing pretty well until the X-rays mixed him up a bit. However, they confused Dr. Donovan too for a few hours.

Robbie Peake goes back to Ethan Allen so I won't see him. He has phoned every day though, and Cam is back from Africa & about to go to China on the same kind of job.

Mother is going to Wash. tomorrow to be with Dad a few days. She'll meet me in N.Y.C. on Monday probably. It's so difficult to get to Baby's Hospital (167th & Broadway) and since I can't help Robbie any I'm not going to try and see him every day. It's easy to phone and the nurses are so fine I don't need to check up on them at all. I'm hoping one of them will come home with him for a week to get him started right. He'll probably need very careful feeding for a while. He may be home by the time you come. Won't that be a thrill?

Don't worry about expense yet. I've managed the Greenwich Hosp. bill, Dr. Knowlton & Greenwich nurses so far out of my allowance, and still have some money left.

Larry and Georgia are fine. Some day while Robbie's still at the hospital I'm going to take Georgia in to the clinic there and find out what's wrong with her skin or blood to get those spots. She's talking a good deal more now. You'll be surprised.

You surely thrilled the girls Christmas. I think they'd like to write and thank you but are embarrassed. I gave them each a raise so they are getting $80.00 now. It seems like a ridiculous amount but when they can get jobs in the city where they have 70^a heat and easy communication with friends & amusements at $100.00 to $125.00 and are willing to stay with me, I guess I'll have to do it. They are so darn nice too. Both of them have been in tears with me a couple of times over Robbie.

Good night darling. I must say I feel ten years younger tonight. Isn't it strange how those tiny bits of life mean the world & all to us the second they get here?

Yours as always.
Peggy

[To George]
[Handwritten, probably on 1/9/43, postmarked on 1/9/43 at 1:30 PM]
[From Greenwich, CT to Fort Leavenworth, KS]

Darling,

Everything seems to be going all right here again. We'll keep our fingers crossed. Robbie is improving every day. I haven't seen him, but I talk to the nurses every day. He cries because they can't feed him enough to satisfy him, but that's because a full tummy might burst the sutures for a few days yet. After tomorrow he'll get a fairly good meal every three hours. You may be here to drive him home with me. That would be even a greater thrill than when Pete brought us both home. I really never expected to make the return trip with Robbie when we took him in Sunday.

Georgia and Larry are grand. We walked up to the farm yesterday morning. It was icy all the way and cold as it could be. The children had great fun slipping and falling on the road, but all of a sudden I found myself flat and failed to see the humor of it. They went into peals of laughter and danced around me singing "Momie fell down." I'm stiff as a board this morning, and have decided I'm getting old for sure now. We saw the pigs after much difficulty. They were all huddled indoors for warmth, I guess. Larry observed "the pigs can't even say Oink! oink! today, Momie." Then we saw the chickens. Two flew right up on the wire netting and clucked at us which gave no end of enjoyment. Next came the swans which are penned up for winter. Doxie got them all excited and the children stood and hissed back at them until I thought my nose was frozen. The weather doesn't improve the old birds' dispositions any. They seem to resent life in general the year round. We ended up in the cow barn to get warm and please Georgia. She makes over these filthy beasts as I'd like her to do over her dolls. Perhaps she'll be a dairy maid—no doubt the type of "Bessie."

Incidentally, I'm reading the best book now. It's Lloyd Douglas' new one called "The Robe."[96] The setting is Rome just prior to the death of Christ & the story concerns a roman soldier who took Christ to be crucified and won his robe at a gambling with the other soldiers. Sounds queer, but it's very good and was rated by N.Y.T. Sunday book section as the most widely read book from coast to coast last week.

Miss O'Riley just phoned and Robin is fine, but still

---

[96] Douglas, Lloyd C. *The Robe*. Boston: Houghton Mifflin, 1942.

hungry. She said all she worries about is spoiling him. Today she can pick him up for the first time since the operation and she can hardly wait to get her hands on him. She claims he knows her voice which I'm sure he does and is so cute every time she talks to him. It almost made me want to catch the first train in.

Did you think I am still considering Lake Placid? Darling, that was before this operation. My only desire now is to get Robin well and the bills paid.

Mother went to Washington on Thurs. and will meet me in N.Y.C. Monday. She was just beaming in anticipation of seeing Dad when she left. Of course the strain has been terrific on her too the last ten days, but most of it was just the thrill of seeing him. I do hope they'll have each other many more years. I've noticed lately that they love us and worry about us and our children but what really matters most is each other which is as it should be.

In all the rush of my letters lately I forgot to tell you that the Sun. after Christmas Peter Hite came out for a cocktail with the Browns. He's a Lieut J.G.[97] in the Coast guard about to go to school in Miami. He hasn't changed a bit. Did his best to find out all your business arrangements and figures and estate taxes, but it was nice to see him. Brown's greeting to me was also typical. He glanced at my chest and said "I see the new one eats well." The Bowdins, Haggsons, & Mom & Dad were there. I don't know how many heard him. They brought their little boy (2 yrs) along and Georgia took him in hand. First she turned herself inside out to show off. Then picked a fight which ended in cracking their skulls together. She laughed and he cried.

Must get this to the mail man. I'm certainly fixed as far as driving gas now. Good I like my own company. Yours

Peggy

---

[97] J.G. is the abbreviation for Junior Grade, used primarily for officers in the Navy or Coast Guard who rank below a lieutenant but above an ensign. It is the equivalent of a first lieutenant in the other branches of the Armed Forces.

[To Peggy]
[Handwritten, probably 1/11/43, postmarked 1/11/43 at 5 PM]
[From Fort Leavenworth, KS to Greenwich, CT]

Peg dear,

It is a nice sunny day, no snow, and not too cold. I just finished lunch and am at my desk from where I can look out across the ridges to the south. Someone sitting erect and easy in the saddle is just cantering a horse across the top of the nearest ridge, which made me think you must be missing Stepson now that you are back to normal again.

Sorry to miss you on the phone yesterday, but I was mighty glad to know that Robbie was coming along well. Don't be too anxious to take him home, if anything should develop from the operation they could take so much better care of it in a hospital.

They are running a Civilian Army Orientation class here now for about 100 businessmen[98] with Minnesota well represented by

---

[98] A handful of orientation courses were provided to American businessmen, journalists, and industrialists to help them, as prominent civilians, better understand and appreciate the various problems facing the military as well as encourage support for solutions. Notable attendees included Roy E. Larsen, President of *Time* magazine and Philip K. Wrigley of the Wm Wrigley Company in Chicago (TYL 1951, 17).

Stanley Lyman, C.P. Joffrey, Walter McCarthy, and one of the Vice Pres. from Gen Mills. I found they were all in the same apartment and stopped in to say hello, but they were all out so I am going over tonight. There is a George Garret from Washington on the list also, a partner in Alph Beane's firm.

I sure wished that I was walking up to the farm with you yesterday. Matter of fact I wouldn't mind loving you in my arms right this minute. Pleased to know you are getting all dressed up for me, you better be looking fine.

Much love dear
George

[To Peggy]
[Handwritten, probably on 1/14/43, postmarked on 1/14/43 at 5 PM]
[From Fort Leavenworth, KS to Greenwich, CT]

Peg dear,

Just a quick note to let you know I am still thinking about you. You really are a very difficult person for me to get along without.

There is not very much news today, except that I love you very much, which is not very much news. Just like back in college I am counting the days until I can see you again.

The work is going good, the returned papers all satisfactory. It is really interesting, most of it [is] problems of various forces laid on maps, the Reds opposed by the blues. Quite a bit like an involved game of chess without such fixed rules on the moves, which in each case must be computed on the basis of the time, space, terrain, type of equipment, and supplies available. The director of the WAACs Col Hobby[99] spoke to us day before yesterday, a charming personality,

---

[99] Oveta Culp Hobby was the Director of the Women's Army Auxiliary Corps (WAACs). "A competent, efficient woman," Col. Hobby had the political acumen necessary to navigate War Department politics and the poise of a traditional American "lady," inspiring other women to join the WAACs and "free a man for combat" (HAM 1991-1995, 5).

but I still do not know what they will do with all of them.[100]

I will get in[to] N.Y. Sunday Jan 31 at 5$\frac{40}{}$ A.M., so I will see you some time Sunday morning. Have to go to class now.

My love dear
George.

---

[100] The WAAC was created to work alongside the Army (but not as a fully integrated or equal part) initially so women could fill various essential service and communications jobs enabling more men to fight overseas. However, by the end of WWII, over 150,000 American women had served in the WAAC in a wide variety of positions. Their responsibilities ranged from manning aircraft warning stations to issuing weapons and processing soldiers to working as cryptographers, parachute riggers, mail sorters, equipment field testers, and even as crew members aboard B-17 training flights. A handful of women were also involved in the Manhattan Project (HAM 1991-1995, 3, 4, 12, 13).

[To George]
[Handwritten, undated[101]]
[Locations unknown]

Darling,

I'm about to feed Robin and crawl into bed, but I wanted to talk to you a while first. How I wish I could be snuggled into your arms and gossip into your ear that way tonight instead of writing it all. This is pretty good though and reading my nonsense is a surer way of knowing you hear me. Your mind cannot wander to better things. Doxie and I have been curled up in your green chair in front of the fire with me reading "This Above All"[102] until a few minutes ago. Before that Larry and Georgia had dinner at the table with Momie tonight. I sat in your chair with Georgia on my left & Larry in my chair. We ate meatloaf, mashed potatoes & gravy, squash and had frozen strawberries for dessert. Then Momie showed the new movies which are marvelous except that one shot of you & the kids which I'm still sick over. My audience was most appreciative and loved Grandma falling in the snow. That roll is good of all of us. After the show Tina & Anna left for the movies and the children went to bed

---

[101] Peggy was looking for houses during February 1943 but this letter may be misplaced.

[102] Knight, Eric *This Above All*. United Kingdom: Cassell, 1941.

so that's when Doxie and I settled down to the fire.

I needed the fire too as I spent the afternoon looking at Greenwich houses for sale and rent with Pinky Boissivain.[103] They are all closed and freezing. After one day of hunting here are my first impressions. I cannot rent a house for what I pay here. To get anything near town which will hold us I must pay $175.00 to $225.00 per month and they aren't in any better condition upon first glance at least. To buy a place just large enough for us for the duration meaning 3 bedrooms 2 baths 1 maids room—no library $20,000. is the least for a place of modern construction. On the other hand, some enormous places—new gorgeous grounds everything in perfect shape and luxuriously built are very little more but these are too much for me to cope with without you and with the help problem what it is. Also, they naturally are not convenient to town. These, though are the bargains and _not_ the small houses. And the small houses are fine for me now but they wouldn't take all our furniture and would not be what we'd want after the war if our standard of living is at all comparable to what it is now. I'm

---

[103] It is possible this last name is spelled wrong by the editor.

not through looking though but Pinky felt that my impression was fairly accurate.

Tomorrow (Wed) I'm going to N.Y.C. with Marjorie & Bernice & Helen Gorton. We're going to Louis & Armand's for lunch and to [the] "Dough Girls" matinée.[104] Then Marjorie & I are staying overnight at the Ambassador & I'll see Dr. Wing Thurs. a.m. & maybe Alice Happel if she hasn't gone home. I'll be home Thurs. afternoon.

It was swell to hear from you this morning. Now I'm looking for news that you'll be here Sunday. I half told Larry you might come and now he asks each morning if it's Sunday yet.

Must get Robin. It's nearly 11.00. I have a swell surprise for you when you get here too.

Yours as always
Peggy

---

[104] *The Doughgirls*, a comedy play written by Joseph Fields, debuted at the Lyceum Theatre in New York City on December 30, 1942. It was incredibly successful, giving 671 performances, the last of which was in late July 1944 (PB n.d.). It was turned into a movie which premiered in November 1944.

[To George]
[Handwritten, probably 2/23/43]
[Locations unknown]

Darling,

We're home again safe and sound, but tired and lonesome for you. The twenty minute late start we had followed me all day. Larry and his Teddy took your place in my bed after you left and we never woke up until [a] quarter to nine. We dashed to dress and pack, couldn't get a taxi, had to go without breakfast that Elizabeth [had] fixed and then get her to drive us to make the train at 9:38. Believe it or not, we did make it too and then it was late. Poor Elizabeth and John. I guess they never dreamed houseguests could be so much trouble. Try and get them to drive over for dinner when John gets back. The phone was 4-6704 I believe.

Again Larry and I missed by 10 seconds having to join the crowds in the train aisles. As it was so filthy, smelly and smokey we were exhausted when we got here.

You'll be glad to know I made an extensive search and located the car registrations etc in my raincoat pocket.

During the search I found this letter from Jessie under the Oldsmobile seat. I hesitated to enclose it for fear it would make you feel badly, but I also know if it were my mother I should enjoy seeing it. Tell me if I'm not right. It's a very sweet letter and very typical of Jessie.

I'm about to unpack my suitcase, take a bath and crawl into bed.

I'll also enclose a letter I found waiting for us here from Ansie Moore.

The other children are fine. Georgia was so thrilled to see Larry it was very touching and Robin has gained over half a pound!

All my love dear and many thanks for the many new memories I can add to my cherished collection from these last few days.

Peggy

P.S. Cannot find your checks but I've sent a note to Miss Finn to send you some.

[To George]
[Handwritten, probably on 2/25/43, postmarked on 2/26/43 at 11 AM]
[From Greenwich, CT to Rome, NY[105]]

Darling

Whew!! I just finished my exercises and crawled into bed exhausted. You should hear me puffing. I wish you'd hurry and come home so I can let my poor figure relax. This is terrible. For dinner tonight I had sauerkraut & pork chops (no spareribs anymore)[106] and they were so good that I wished even more than usual that you could have shared dinner with me. Since dinner I've played the piano for about an hour and a half and now at 8:30 I'm in bed talking to you. Then I'm going to read 'This Above All' which I

---

[105] Rome, NY was the home of the former Griffiss Air Force Base, established on February 1, 1942. Until it was renamed in 1948 after the first US airman to die in the European theater (Townsend Griffiss), the base had 12 different names, among which was the Rome Air Depot Control Area Command, its name while George was there. If referenced further, it will be called the Rome Air Depot (RAD) for its simplicity. During the war, RAD's main mission was to provide aircraft engine maintenance and repair as well as to train air depot groups in aircraft engine maintenance (MUE 1989, 205, 208).

[106] Hoarding and rush buying were common problems during WWII, resulting in shortages on everyday items in grocery stores throughout the country. Meat shortages were already commonplace by mid-January 1943 and most shoppers were forced to choose from what remained after these rushes on the stores. It is possible spareribs were among the items unavailable when Peggy shopped (NYT 01/15/1943, 14L). Meat rationing would begin several weeks after this letter, on March 29, 1943.

borrowed from the Peters. Then I'll give Robbie his bottle and go to sleep. The girls have gone out and it's so quiet. I long for these evenings with you but I manage to pass them without feeling too sorry for myself so don't worry. Furthermore I don't get into any mischief such as throwing away your treasured scraps of paper as you used to complain about.

I took Robin to the Dr. today and he was 12lb 14oz. a gain of 2 1/2 lbs in a month. Dr Close thought it was remarkable even without the 10 days of diarrhea when he didn't gain at all. We also got our # 2 ration books today.[107] It seems of as if there's enough red tape to buying food now to almost make fasting a good habit to acquire.[108] Maybe

---

[107] Officially called War Ration Book no. 2, this book of ration stamps was issued when point-rationing of processed foods began on March 1, 1943. Point rationing is a way to ration related items within a group that can be interchanged for the same number of points. It was later used for meat rationing as well (HOL 1943, 44). In order to obtain Book no. 2, a member of each household had to show each Book no. 1 to the Ration Board. They then needed to show a properly filled out consumer declaration form, listing, among other things, how many 8oz. cans, bottles, and jars they had as well as how many pounds of coffee they had at home so that the proper number of stamps could be deducted.

[108] Peggy is not exaggerating. By the time point rationing arrived, Americans had already needed to learn two other systems of rationing. The first was coupon rationing, introduced in spring 1942, which was used to ration specific, single commodities; for example, sugar and gasoline were both rationed this way. War Ration Book no. 1 was an important part of the coupon rationing system. Technically, there were two types of coupon rationing: uniform coupon rationing, which meant that consumers all received equal shares of an item (everyone received 2lbs. of sugar per month, for example) and differential coupon rationing

that's where Gandhi is smart.

The weather has been very mild since last Sat. and by the time Larry and I arrived the snow was all gone. Today I spent the morning pruning the bushes at the back of the garage. Whatever is done I'll have to do so I'd better start early. It would be much more fun if I could do it on our own place. But then I think how much more fun it's going to be to do it on our own place with you.

I have an appointment next Tuesday to see what else is available here for renting. Mr. Ryan is really impossible

---

where single products were rationed based on the varying needs of consumers (gasoline is a good example as delivery drivers needed more gasoline than an office worker). The second option was rationing through use of a purchase certificate. This was used for items such as automobiles, rubber, and heating stoves and had begun in most parts of the country by the beginning of January 1942 with the rationing of tires. Obtaining a purchase certificate involved a visit to one's local Rationing Board, filling out forms with necessary information demonstrating a need for the requested item, waiting for an approval, and waiting to receive said certificate in order to make the purchase (HOL 1943, 44).

Point rationing, the third system, was especially confusing as each point corresponded to a ration value, a value that was subject to change depending on the economics of supply and demand. The point rationing system was complicated and many grocery stores had volunteer "explainers" present to assist confused shoppers. In an attempt to help, products were also marked with their ration value as well as their price value and cashiers were to issue receipts with both sets of numbers available (NYT 03/01/1943, 13). Also adding to the confusion was the fact that certain products like sugar and coffee were still covered by Book no. 1. A housewife doing the family shopping would have to manage two separate rationing systems in her head as she tried to make her purchases and women were instructed to plan their grocery lists, complete with ration sticker values for each item, before leaving the house so as to not cause bottlenecks and slowdowns in the grocery stores (BRO 1943, 15).

about everything even though he gets $30.00 a month out of me for eggs and milk. However the latest blow is that after this week the diaper service refuses to come out this far. That really hurts. Helen may come out tomorrow to spend the day and night. Also Marjorie may bring Hodgie up, but nothing is definite. Helen has a cold to get rid of first and Marjorie may have a date in N.Y.C.

Saturday night I'm going to the Buckhauts for dinner. That's pleasure driving but until today the cars haven't been out for over a week. Anyhow I'm going to risk it.

Larry has been a spoiled brat since the weekend. No wonder, I suppose. He won't do anything he's asked too and he refuses to let Tina teach him and she's so nice to him. I don't know why he wants me cause all I do is scold and spank him. It should be O.K. by tomorrow. He was awfully cute too though. He told Anna all about his weekend today. I heard him tell her how "many lot of hugs and kisses" he had for "_my_ Daddy." Georgia chimed in with "No! _My_ Daddy" and the war was on again. "Judy," "Bob" and "Teddy" figured quite prominantly (sp?) also.

It's Anna's weekend off so Sunday you can think of me here with Tina and our tribe. Robin looks wonderfully. You're going to see some difference. How about coming down next weekend? We surely would like to see you.

Jeane's waiting for her baby now. It's two days overdue. As you see by the clipping, Alice has finally produced.

That's about all the news that's "fit to print." The rest is purely confidential. I love you more each day and begrudge each minute of our separation until I'm now considering making a schedule to double the efficiency of each day of our lives after this is all over to make up for now. Do you think we can? For instance all the nights you used to spend on artillery problems will be used for loving me and all the days you went to work we'll spend working together on our farm. All the trips you took alone before you'll pay 2 full fares and 3 half fares for company. Doesn't that sound like a good idea?

Anyway we're all waiting for you.

Peggy

XO Doxie

XXXOOO

l.g.R. l.g.R.

[To Peggy]
[Handwritten, probably on 2/27/43, postmarked on 2/28/43 at 8 PM]
[From Rome, NY to Greenwich, CT]

My darling,

That was certainly a hurried departure last Tuesday morning. I remember hearing the alarm go off and resenting it very much. Guess it was just too nice there with you in my arms to want to ∧do anything foolish like get ∧out of bed and start dressing. As it was I had plenty of time to catch the bus and even got there early enough so that I had a seat and did not have to stand hanging to a strap all the way as on the previous morning.

There has been no further word from up the line about my assignment to a task force staff so maybe Col. Smith's request was effective. If so I will have to come down to have a laugh at your fortune teller.

It has been much warmer her[e] with some of the snow melting but it started snowing again last night. Thursday night I went up skating on the officer's pond but the ice was poor.

Here is a bit of extra confidential news. Col McPike[109] has been ordered over, to leave early next week which will put Col Smith[110] in command of the area as ∧ᵸᵉ ⁱˢ second ranking officer now.

I enjoyed your visit very much, it left so many pleasant moments to cherish. I love you very much my dear. Will write 1st of week about coming down if possible.

Love George

---

[109] Colonel George V. McPike was the first base commander of the Rome Air Depot beginning February 1, 1942 (MUE 1989, 205).

[110] The base commander who followed Colonel McPike was Colonel Donald D. Arnold. He took over on February 5, 1943. Who Colonel Smith was and why he was not made base commander are both unknown (MUE 1989, 205).

[To Peggy]
[Handwritten, postmarked on 3/2/43 at 4:30 PM]
[From Rome, NY to Greenwich, CT]

Darling:

This pen I am using is the one I got up in Miami the day you and Larry left. I like it because you can just dip it in the special no spill ink bottle that goes with it and thus you can write a whole page without dipping it again. I am going to keep it for my desk when the war is over.

Looking back Key West does hold some very pleasant memories too. I have a very pleasant memory of seeing a charming young lady walk up to me at the desk in the lobby of the Columbus Hotel just as I was inquiring about you. That was a delightful trip driving back down the keys with you. Meeting you and Larry on the platform the next trip was one of those bright memories that never fades. That night with the Burtons, Streets, and Maj McMillan[111] was fun. It

---

[111] It is possible that George is writing about Lt. Col. George Bray McMillan who was a Major in 1942 when George was in Key West and promoted to Lt. Col. by the next time George visited him. An Ace who was a member of the American Volunteer Group, better known as the Flying Tigers, Lt. Col. McMillan was stationed at the Army Air Forces Proving Ground at Eglin Field, Florida once he returned from his missions in China. At Eglin he flew a variety of

will be good to see them all again someday, and of course I would like to see Don Morrell. Moments I spend with you always seem to turn into treasured memories my dear, and that little narrow bed we shared at the Atwoods won't soon be forgotten either, nor some precious moments that Friday night in Utica. Each time we are together I think I love you more than ever before. And friends I can share with you always come to be closer than the ones you do not meet. I am so proud to have my friends meet you. Darling I love you so very much. And I do appreciate all these trips you have made to come see me. But I do keep longing for the time when we can be together all the time.

Now to be a bit more practical, I would like to have you make a list of all the medical expenses we have had during 1942 and send them to Miss Finn. There is a new provision in the federal income tax law which allows these as deductions.[112] Will you do this so that

---

fighters and improved his flying skills. He returned to China where his aircraft was shot down, killing him, in June 1944 (FOR 2016).

[112] In early 1943, the federal government announced that many medical expenses could be counted as deductions on a person's federal income tax form. Expenses included that Peggy and George could benefit from deducting were diagnosis, treatment, and hospitalization— both for Peggy and again for Robin's later surgery (NYT 02/09/1943, 18). The deductions provided some relief for Americans who found themselves paying more than ever before for

Miss Finn can get our tax return in by March 15.

I am not sure that I can get away this weekend but will wire you as soon as I know for sure. I am hoping to get down to New York Saturday night though.

It sounded as though you had your hands full Sunday morning. I wished very much that I was there.

With much love
George.

_____

their income taxes, as the normal tax rate jumped from four to six percent. Some Americans paid an increase six times larger than the previous year (ENR 1943, 10).

[To George]
[Handwritten, probably on 3/8/43, postmarked on 3/9/43 at 11:30 AM]
[From Greenwich, CT to Rome, NY]

Darling,

Just listened to Gabriel Heatter[113] and am wondering what Stalin will do about Admiral Standley's complaint of Russia's non recognition of U.S. aid.[114] Looks more and more

---

[113] Gabriel Heatter was a radio newsman known for his optimism, emphasis on good news, and ability to find believable silver linings to reassure his listeners that everything would be all right again (NYT 03/31/1972, 32).

[114] Admiral William H. Standley was the United States Ambassador to the Soviet Union. On March 8, 1943, frustrated with a lack of progress in the exchange of information between the U.S. and Soviet governments, Standley remarked to reporters that he believed information on the extent to which the U.S. was supplying the Russians with aid through Lend-Lease, the Red Cross, and the Russian-American relief was being concealed from the Russian people (by deliberate omission in the Soviet press) with the intent to create the illusion the Soviets were fighting the war alone. Previously, Stalin had expressed frustration with Churchill and Roosevelt's military presence in Africa rather than opening a second front in Europe to aid the Red Army and had remarked that, "the Red Army alone is bearing the whole weight of the war." With the House of Representatives preparing to vote on an extension of the Lend-Lease package the next day, Standley argued that, "it is not fair to mislead Americans into giving millions from their pockets, thinking that they are aiding the Russian people, without the Russian people knowing about it." He continued, cautioning that, "It is a long way from the Foreign Affairs Committee to enactment" (TUP 03/09/1943, 1,5). Unfortunately for Standley, his remarks were not well-received by American officials, many of whom pointed to multiple articles in Pravda (the official Soviet paper), in addition to other periodicals, not only listing Lend-Lease items and amounts received, but also printing transcripts of Churchill and Roosevelt's speeches about their Lend-Lease commitments and agreements, illustrating the Russian people were well aware of where the support was coming from. Stalin and the Soviets responded to Standley's comments by airing the most recent statement from the U.S. Lend-Lease Administrator, Edward Stettinius Jr., where all of the aid provided to Britain and the Soviet Union by the United States was listed (HUL 1943, 1,5).

as if fighting for the peace is going to be just as difficult as winning the war.

Our house is in order again tonight. Mondays are certainly busy here. I take care of Robin and do the washing while Anna cleans and Tina takes care of Larry and Georgia and cleans her 3 rooms.

I kept Larry in bed again today, but I'll let him up tomorrow. He was nauseated this morning but his fever had broken. This was the craziest ailment. Dr. Close said he'd seen a lot of it in the past week and said the children showed few symptoms but the fever and a mild sore throat. It's some virus that's going around. As you probably realized he didn't feel very badly.

In fact I even did go out last night for a few hours to the Bridge's. We had a drink and then a long argument on what's too be done for preparing a proper peace after the war. As usual I get hot whenever I hear "Oh that's easy, we've got to annihilate all germans and Japs." Ann said that so Joe and I jumped all over her for three hours, ~~but~~ but she still thinks they all must die. -----! It's discouraging when even among a few people of our own class and education there is such narrow mindedness and bitter opposition. The boys in this war must stick it out and see a decent, intelligent, peace made. We don't want Larry and Georgia and Robin going through this when they are our age.

Did I tell you Jeane had a baby girl Thurs. night? They've named her Betty Beane. Poor Jeane and Alph. They wanted a boy so badly.

I can hardly wait to see you Saturday. Be sure and let me know what time you get into Harmon.

Think over what we can give to Red Cross this year. I was called today and said I'd let them know Monday after talking to you.

I haven't heard from Frank or Helen so guess they aren't back yet. I had lunch with Mrs. Bigelow Thurs. at Savoy.

Bring down the case of gin, if you can. Also your laundry and any socks that need mending.

I'm looking forward to Saturday night—and Sunday. Yours always—I love you so very much

Peggy

[To Peggy]
[Handwritten, postmarked on 3/29/43 at 12 AM]
[From Rome, NY to Greenwich, CT]

My darling:

It was good to hear your voice, and a pleasant surprise to speak to our little boy. I am sorry he is sick, but I was proud to hear how nicely he spoke over the phone.

Mrs. Smith is very nice, but she just makes me realize once more what a wonderful, capable, young lady I married. You have so much poise, are so able and considerate, and the sweetest girl in the world.

I do love you very very much, and hope it will not be too long before we can be together all the time,

Yours
George.

[To Peggy]
[Handwritten,[115] probably on 5/7/43, postmarked on 5/8/43 at 6:30 AM]
[From Miami, FL to Greenwich, CT]

Peg dear:

Got down here all right last night. Uncle George was at the station to meet us and Capt. Hestad and I went out for dinner and spent the night. Today we went over to the Bath club for a swim, then to Indian Creek for lunch. Good hearted Uncle George picked up a lovely looking Naval doctor and took him along. We came in town checked our baggage the P.M. went over to see Maj (now lt Col) McMillan who had to work tonight so could not come to dinner. Walters and Lovenbury (both from Manchester and now majors) are working in the same headquarters. Called Morrell and found him just going off on leave. They all sent you their regards.

Tonight we went over to Alworth's for cocktails and then Mr. & Mrs. Alworth came back over to Momie and Georges for dinner. Had many pleasant memories of our visit here in 1940, slept in the same room. That certainly is a lovely set up, the weather is just

---

[115] On The Columbus Hotel stationery included in Memories.

perfect here now. Leave the hotel tomorrow $4^{\underline{30}}$ AM for 36th St Air Port and take off at $6^{\underline{00}}$ AM.

I have made reservations for the 26th to get me in N.Y. by noon of the 27th of May. Reservations are _very_ hard to get from here north so that is why I did that. If you plan to go to Mpls that is perfectly all right, but please let me know what your plans are. You can write me at the Columbus Hotel and mark "_Please Hold_" I would have to leave early on the morning of the 30th of May from Greenwich. So I would have about 2 1/2 days at home. Of course the weather down here might interfere. At any rate I will wire you as soon as we land here.

I love you very much dear.

George

[To Peggy]
[Handwritten, probably on 5/9/43, postmarked on 5/13/43]
[From unknown location[116] to Greenwich, CT]

Darling:

Arrived safely after rather a tedious trip. It has been raining ever since we arrived. The quarters are good, and from first impression, the officers we will be with are very capable and willing to help us. Of course it is quite warm here.

Hope everything is going well about the house. I will be back up there before June 1, so I may be able to help you out. Hardly seems possible that I was home last Sunday. It was a short but much enjoyed visit. Any mail that comes to the house you had best hold for me.

Thought of you today on 'Mothers Day' sorry I could not remind your children to send flowers. You might take a look at our tennis racquets, if we do get a chance to play it might be well to have them restrung.

---

[116] In a letter from Peggy's father, included in Additional Letters, he mentions George taking a trip to the West Indies. It is possible that George was sent to one of the island countries that makes up the West Indies but this has not been confirmed.

Guess I have not really got much to say but I just wanted to write you a letter. After two years of not living with you I don't know how I am going to last out, but guess we will make out some way. I just hope it will not be too much longer.

All my love
George

Say hello to Larry and Georgia and give young Robin a kiss.

[To Peggy]
[Handwritten, probably on 5/14/43, postmarked 5/15/43 --M]
[From unknown location to Greenwich, CT]

Dear Peggy:

Thought you might like a letter tonight. Maj Ream and I just got back from an early movie after dinner. It was not too good "Orchestra Wives."[117] A way back when we used to live together I hardly ever saw a movie. Guess there were always too many interesting ways to spend an evening with you to bother with a movie. Now I go quite often.

I ran into Lt. Morriss who was in Blake[118] with me, and also a fellow by the name of Raymond who was at Yale when I was and now is an Army M.D. Morriss is in the Coast Artillery and did a swell job of explaining their setup here to us.

Down by the water today I noticed a surf board and some sail boats which made me think of how I would like to drive up to Thunder Lake with you for about a month this summer. Maybe

---

[117] *Orchestra Wives* was released in September 1942 and starred Ann Rutherford and George Montgomery.

[118] The Blake School is a private, preparatory day school in Minneapolis, MN.

next summer. Hope someone gets some pleasure out of that place, perhaps Helen and Frank might want to go up there for awhile.

The temperature stays just about the same here every day around $80°$ and it is cloudy all the time with intermittent showers.

I have been wondering what you might be doing tonight, out for dinner and cards, perhaps Round Hill, or maybe home playing the piano. Wish I were with you whatever it is. I just don't seem to get used to not being with you.

My love dear, George.

[To Peggy]
[Handwritten on 5/19/43, postmarked on 5/20/43 at 4 PM]
[From unknown location to Greenwich, CT]

Dear Peggy:

We will be in Miami next Tuesday night. If you have not gone out West I will catch a train Wednesday morning getting me in New York Thursday noon. I will call the Savoy Plaza in case you are in town, so you might leave a message there if you are in town. I have to get back down to Norfolk by Sunday evening as we have to be on duty there Monday A.M.

Have been well, busy, and interested, but still had plenty of time to miss you. Of course I have been wondering where you went and what you did when you were here. Can't say as this would be too good a place to pick for a pleasure visit, unless it was a short one.

It is a beautiful night here though. A full moon that is very bright. There are a bunch of boys singing over in one of the barracks. The frogs are joining in with a chorus of their own. The last couple of days the weather has improved. It was been clear most all day but not too hot. We spent most of the day out in the jungle.

Wish I could be with you on your birthday. I am thinking of the nice way you gave me a ring for mine, and wish I could do the same for you. Remind me some time and ~~I will~~ perhaps I can arrange it. I do miss you so very much dear,

All my love George.

Memories

The COLUMBUS

MIAMI · FLORIDA

Darling:

Wish I had had my hair cut
before you left. I stopped in a barber
shop on the way back and I sure needed
one. I had quite a talk with the barber
who came from Salerno, Italy, on the
Bay of Naples. We stopped there remember,
He believed in state socialism when
I went in, but thought Mussolini and
Hitler were terrible. I hope I changed
his mind.

The room looks awful empty now

MIAMI'S FINEST BAYFRONT HOTEL

MRS. GEORGE R. STEINER - NORTH STREET - GREENWICH, CONNECTICUT

Mon.

My darling,

So much will have happened by
the time you receive this letter that
it's almost foolish to try and write,
but I am too worried to get busy at
housework and it seems a comfort
just to talk to you like this. Your
letter written New year's Eve and New
year's arrived this morning and I read
it while walking along the snow on
North St to Conyers for vegetables. It
almost seemed as if you were with
me and I was so thrilled to know
you love me as much this year
as last.

I have just talked to Dr Donovan
over the phone and he says there is
no need for any further observation. Robbie

HOTEL PENNSYLVANIA   NEW YORK

Monday

Darling:

Just thought I might just as well tell you that I love you, so long as I have to address an envelope anyway. Wish you were in here with me tonight. A hotel is kind of a lonely place. Guess I will never want to be a traveling salesman, it would be too lonely.

Give Larry and Georgia's his from Daddy. That number was Hempstead 881. It is the Headquarters of the First Air Service Area Command (I ASA)

Love George

KANSAS

Monday

Dearest,

Now it is Monday morning, the first week and eight more to go. They really keep us busy. Four hours of conferences in the morning, four in the afternoon plus another hour of optional instruction which is one of those affairs that everyone finds expediant to attend. Then you are encouraged not to study after eleven. Breakfast is 6^{30} class at 8^{00} so with 30 minutes for walking to breakfast and to class 20 minutes for breakfast I still have about 40 minutes left all to myself in which I can write you. So that will give you a

Sunday

My darling Peggy,

Your voice sounded so good today. I think you must have been very pleased to have Irene and George there with you today. I certainly wish that I could have been part of that party. Are they duely impressed with Robbie and Miss Georgia and Master Larry. I tell you I feel mighty proud every time I think of them which is often.

I have a little picture here on the

Captain George Steiner

Georgia, Peggy, and Larry

Georgia, George, and Larry

House on Oakley Lane, Greenwich, CT – shortly before George was shipped overseas

Larry, Peggy, and Georgia

Larry, Georgia and George at the farmhouse they rented, 1941

Larry, George, Georgia, and Doxie (winter 1943)

EPILOGUE

George is abruptly sent overseas in June 1943. The second volume of this collection will contain the letters Peggy and George wrote each other while George was stationed in Algiers, Algeria and Peggy was either in Greenwich, CT or at her parents' lake house on Crystal Bay in Minnesota.

AFTERWORD

This project began on a nondescript day in Chicago, when I abruptly fell walking across the street. "Would you believe," my Mom said when I called her after my urgent care visit, "that your Grandma's friend, Georgia, just did the same thing to her foot?" I sent Georgia a get-well card and introduced myself. And there we were: two strangers laid up in our respective beds with our feet up.

Perhaps the most challenging part for Georgia and me was the exasperation at having to sit still (a lifelong struggle for Georgia) while "to-do" lists grew longer. Georgia recovered rapidly but my injury saw me return home to stay with my Mom and Grandma for over a month while my Mom supervised the prescribed "sitting still and staying off the foot" period.

While at home, I met Georgia in person. She asked me if I would like to help her with a project. Her parents, she explained, had written hundreds of letters to each other during WWII and the letters were sitting in her office. The letters needed to be sorted, placed in chronological order, and scanned.

I began reading the letters in order to get a better sense of what was happening in the lives of the writers. During this process I discovered that many of the letters were undated, but thankfully the context of the letters' content allowed me to place them in their proper chronological sequence. I passed the especially touching letters on to my Mom who sat on the floor with me, reading all of them as I placed them back in the boxes. It was during one of these reading sessions (although admittedly it was more crying and chuckling than reading) that my Mom commented on how nice it would be for the letters to be published in a book so they could be shared with others.

While my Mom was laughing and crying along with Peggy and George, I was more interested in the history of the time period. I researched the events and people mentioned in the letters, and then thought it would be nice if one were able to read the letters and have basic information accessible in the form of footnotes. However, nearing the end of the project, I realized that I, too, had become invested in the experiences of Georgia's parents when I called Georgia demanding (half panicked) to know what had happened to Doxie, the family dog. I was outraged the letters ended without telling me the fate of Peggy's beloved companion. The several days it took Georgia to remember Doxie's story were agonizing and it was at that point I understood my Mom's insistence on the story having a broad appeal.

We suggested the book idea to Georgia and she was thrilled. Of course, none of us realized what creating a book entailed. What we did know was that Georgia's parents had eloquently written their lives into the larger history of WWII.

We hope you have found Peggy and George's letters as compelling as we have.

ACKNOWLEDGMENTS

It was a privilege to work with all of the original letters and photographs in this collection. An enormous thank you to Georgia for making them available to me. I have appreciated your willingness to share your family with me and I've enjoyed listening to your stories.

During this project, a couple of individuals stand out for being above and beyond friendly and helpful. Thank you to Joe R. Bailey at Fort Leavenworth for the information on George's program at the Command and General Staff School. I enjoyed our several conversations and appreciated your recommendations and sources. Nothing is more overwhelming than all of the things I do not know, so I am especially appreciative of Prof. Nicole Phelps for her willingness to answer questions and provide suggestions when I had doubts about what I was doing.

A handful of motivated individuals helped greatly with everything from reading early drafts to suggesting rewordings and rewrites. Thank you and a big hug to the lovely Chrissie Williams for her thorough read of the first full draft. I appreciate how many little inconsistencies you found. Thank you to fabulous Jo Williams as well, because "interned" should never be "interred" and I'm so glad you not only pulled out a dictionary, but you brought it to my attention. Thank you to C. Farinella, Cynthia, and Carmen for your close reads as well. Your feedback was much appreciated and I enjoyed hearing your own family stories and your unique reactions to the book. Thank you to Dave for his beautiful covers and his patience throughout the process.

I am grateful for my bestie extraordinaire, Dr. Marisa Fontana. From letting me toss ideas around with you to checking excerpts I wrote were coherent, you always picked up the phone when I called. This project would have been much less fun, and a lot more frustrating without you.

Thank you to Andre for enthusiastically accompanying me to libraries, coffeeshops, bookstores, and everywhere else I went while researching and writing.

Someone needs to live in the present day and I am especially lucky that my wonderful husband Agustin understands the real world well enough to keep its distractions from me. Thank you for making sure bills were paid on time and dinner was made so that I was able to focus solely on this project. It sounds mundane but making me dinner is the kindest thing anyone could ever do for me and I love you so much for accepting that about me!

This project would not have been possible without the love and support of my Mom. From the original idea to plans "a" through "w," you were as much a part of this as I was. Thank you for diligently tracking down missing letters. Thank you for making friends with Apple's support team. Thank you for your motivation, support, and for advocating for me and this project wherever and whenever you can. Thank you for answering the phone at all hours of the day and night, even though you knew the first words out of my mouth would be, "Mom can you read this over real fast and tell me how it sounds?" Thank you for understanding and forgiving me when you picked up the phone and I forgot to say hello or if I hung up without saying I love you. Now it's in print so you can't forget: I love you very much. Thank you for all that you do.

ADDITIONAL LETTERS

[To Peggy and George from Peggy's father]
[Handwritten note and typed letter from 7/28/42, postmarked on 7/28/42 at 4 PM]
[From Minneapolis, MN to Greenwich, CT]

P.S. to Peggy —

Dear Peggy:

Laura took pen in hand to write this letter for me. I thought as long as I was telling George all the news, that I might as well have an extra copy made and send it to you.

I want you to know that I did enjoy my little stay with you. I am looking forward to you returning the visit in Minneapolis.

My love to the kids, and a pat for Doxie.

Love—

Dad—

Captain George R. Steiner
Meacham Field
Key West, Florida

Dear George:

I received another package yesterday from Key West containing a nice box of El Patio cigars. I am enjoying smoking one of them as I dictate this letter. They are exceptionally nice cigars and I appreciate them, as well as the box of Havanas that you sent a couple of weeks ago.

I was in Canada all last week, and on my return found notice to the effect that we are also in receipt of a case containing a dozen and a half cans of turtle soup. I also found that Irene had moved to the Lake. The soup was delivered to the town house, so in the few days to date that I have been home we haven't tried the soup, but I know it will be wonderful. It is fine to have you keep me in cigars, but I don't think you should pay the grocery bill too. I would appreciate if you would tell me the price of the soup so that I can remit. I really think you should do this.

As Peggy has undoubtedly written you, I was in the East the week of the 13th, and spent from 10:30 Thursday night until noon Saturday with your family in Greenwich. They are sure a fine lot, and I sure enjoyed the chance to be with them. Your daughter, to show her independence, fell off the porch. Had her wind knocked out, but that was all the damage done. Enjoyed a round of golf with Peggy Friday afternoon at the Round Hill Club. Did myself proud by shooting 93. At dinner we enjoyed the company of the Peters family, and then went to their house and played bridge, and paid.

I got home Sunday evening, and left Monday evening and spent the next week in Canada. Had a meeting with our sales force in Regina. The crop prospect up there is really something. The crop prospect also is mighty good in the United States. North America will have the food to feed the world, if we can move it to them; but there still seem to be several submarines to be pushed out of the way before we can make deliveries as freely and as fast as we would like.

War production in our own plants is pretty fair. Every day we ship a carload of 155 MM shells; about twice a week carloads of 37 MM shot; daily three cars of ships winches; as well as parts of Bofors guns, and underframes of gun carriages. We have just started shipping for the Navy air fields low-down four-wheel-drive tractors to be used on bomber fields for hauling the big planes into and out of hangers, camouflaged areas, etc.

The farm machinery business is being curtailed more and more all the time. Sales for the fiscal year ending October 31 will probably be about 70% of what they were last year, and the program for 1943 looks like about half of 1942.

Washington wants all of the capacity of the factories capable of building war machinery used for that purpose. The tractor and harvestor plants of the farm machinery industry do adapt themselves pretty well for making war

equipment. We have a lot of machinery that will
do precision work. But our implement plants
where plows, harrows, cultivators, etc., are
made, do not have the equipment needed for war
work, and so in order to keep those plants
going it is necessary that we do have some of
that class of work to do. New harrows, plows,
cultivators, etc. can't be used in a big way
without power to pull them. Our dealers can't
continue in business without a line of
machinery to sell. The Department of
Agriculture's food program cannot be carried
through successfully under present condition of
labor shortage without some new machinery. So
it is necessary that there be a minimum
quantity of farm machinery built. Also, it is
important for the manufacturer that he be able
to continue with enough machinery to sell so as
to keep a nucleus of a sales organization, so
that when the war is over we can get
reorganized and doing business without too much
delay. We have reduced our farm machinery sales
force by nearly one-half, and we are using a
lot of those men in the plant manufacturing war
products, to have them available for sales work
when we need it again.

We have had lots of rain this year. The lake
is way up; water going over the Grays Bay dam,
flowing down the Minnehaha creek and over the
Falls, which now look as beautiful as they did
back in Hiawatha's day. The water at our lake
place is clear back where it was when we bought
the place, almost up to the foot of the big
cottonwood trees. The lawn looks fine and the
flowers are beautiful. Only wish there were
some kids out at the lake to help us enjoy
them.

Irene is well. The Pipers are just getting ready for another wedding. Bobby is to marry one of the daughters of Addison Lewis at Long Lake. Jess Wilcox is getting ready to go to Washington to Billy's wedding. Irene reported last night that she just bought four wedding presents, and had two to go.

Peggy told me she was coming home about October 1st to stay through the big party. She and Thelma are running waist to waist. I don't know who will get there first.

Best regards.

Sincerely,
G.L.S

[To Peggy from George Gillette]
[Handwritten[119] on 5/12/43, postmarked 5/12/43 at 3:30 AM]
[From Minneapolis, MN to Greenwich, CT]

Peggy Dear—

It is a long time since I have taken my pen in hand and written to you. I apologize—for I do enjoy your letters so much—Mother and I read them together and get many laughs out of the funny things the kids do—We should have enjoyed attending the circus with them.

It was fine that you and Geo. could have some time together both in Washington and at home—His sojourn in the West Indies will be just a vacation—May be kind of warm at this time of year. I suppose the job down there is to see that nothing happens to the oil supply from the Dutch Guiana refineries—Martinique and Admiral Roberts are a bit in the lime light—Maybe Geo will be temporary Governor of that.

I saw Geo Webster yesterday—His son Henry an Ensign—is on an air plane tender which is to be the Mother ship to a flock of bombers that patrol the West Indies territory—His ship the — Rockaway––. Please tell Geo—If they could meet it would please Mr Webster greatly. His other son Geo. is a Major now. You have probably heard his story. Maybe you know Geo—graduate of Sheettuck—went to U of M. Interested in little but military—became

---

[119] On Minneapolis-Moline stationery

top officer there—enlisted in regular army—as by assigned to a harbor defense at San Francisco—Married the Colonel's daughter— lived with her there few months—assigned to duty on a small island off the pacific coast from Panama some time in 1941—left his wife in San Francisco—Never returned sticks to job and nothing else so far as anyone knows—Don't write—Wife has baby couple years old Geo has never seen. A strange case—All the Websters are fine folks—

At the dentist office Monday met one of Wal's old friends that used to be at our house a lot—Tut Lyman—Now Mrs Mealey— husband died few years ago—Has son in aviation now at Miami—It was one of her brothers Arthur that was killed in the truck drivers (544) strike several years ago—She is looking fine now—Is said to have had tough going.

I finally got a man to work cleaning up the lake place—He lives in Hopkins—I have to furnish transportation to get him out and back— Meant two round trips if I take him—Today I am trying a new stunt. Drove my car to the office (Hopkins) He took it to the lake—is to be back at five for me to drive home—Hope all goes well.

Monday night we took Jack & Thelma out to dinner—their 5th anniversary—Had a swell time—Thursday is Mother's birthday—I don't know what to do for her—She never says she wants anything personal—sometimes a washing Machine—Mangle—Electric iron— never jewelry, clothing or the like. I added to her bank account yesterday so she can get anything she wants—but I bet the cash stays in the bank.

I would like to get down there to see your new home—I bet it is a dandy—I have an idea I know where it is—You remember when we drove home and found the golf club we came home thru a lane parallel to the Merrit Highway—on the side toward Greenwich—You pointed out a house that you said was for sale that seems to me to answer the description I have heard of the one you bought. Have I the right location?

I believe you are wise in making the purchase—Nothing Makes one feel more secure that to own a home—Of course Mother & I would prefer it to be in Hennepin County but Geo's & your reasons for having it in Greenwich are sound.

Geo is more worried over inflation than I am—Probably he has more dollars that would be deflated and from that standpoint more to worry about—but I would only buy a farm anywhere—If I wanted a farm—Not for fear of inflation—If you have a farm & Don't live on it—Have had no experience running any—You really have some thing to worry about—A farm improperly operated can lose money faster than inflation in reasonable degree applied to a reasonable sum.

Farming is a science—Takes brains—equipment& Manpower to operate one successfully—And always a gamble on the weather—Geo has the brains—undoubtedly to do the job right—but should go into it on other than a sideline basis if that operation is to offset the effect of inflation in a big way.

We would like to have you bring Robbie with you when you come—

Think you will feel easier and not be so anxious to hurry home—Let one of the girls take her vacation before you come—bring her with you—The other can take her vacation while you are here—I would like to get all My five grandchildren together.

I expect by this time you have heard from Geo—We would like to hear all about him & what he is doing that you can tell us. Give him our best when you write.

I am going to a luncheon at the Minneapolis Club—Major Rufus Rand—just back from North Africa is to talk. Our side surely trimmed Messrs Hitler Mussolini & Co in great shape in North Africa. And here is Mr Churchill again in Washington—somethin's cooking.

Business holding good—Paying quarterly dividend on preferred shares the 15th—1 62 $^1/_2$ ¢ Mighty hard to get material—Just as much kicking about the Muddle in Washington now as when I was there—

Weather stays cold—trying to get the town house painted—can't even start—Jack has a swell victory garden ready to plant—Mabel left for good yesterday—Mother in tears—She suffers doing her own work but prefers that to the effort necessary to get and train a new one.

Loads of Love—

Dad

ABBREVIATIONS

AAIR   AAIR. 2009. *Aviation Archaeological Investigation and Research.* Accessed September 16, 2019. https://www.aviationarchaeology.com/src/AARmonthly/Sep1 942S.htm.

BEE   Beevor, Antony. 1998. Stalingrad. New York: Viking.

BRI   Brinkley, Douglas, ed. 2003. *World War II The Allied Counteroffensive*, 1942-1945. New York: Times Books.

BRI1   Brinkley, Douglas, ed. 2003. *World War II The Axis Assault,* 1939-1942. Vol. 1. New York: Times Books.

EB   Britannica, Editors of Encyclopaedia. n.d. "Convoy Naval Operations." *Encyclopedia Britannica.* https://www.britannica.com/topic/convoy-naval-operations.

BRO   Brown, Prentiss M. 1943. "How To Make Rationing Work." *The New York Times*, February 21: 15x.

CWS   1941. "Class Report." Unit Gas Officers' Course (Aviation) July 21- August 16, 1941. Chemical Warfare School Edgewood Arsenal.

COF   Coffey, Thomas. 1982. HAP: *The Story of the U.S. Air Force and the Man Who Built It.* New York City: The Viking Press.

DAV   Davis, Anita Price. 2014. *North Carolina and World War II: A Documentary Portrait.* Jefferson: McFarland & Company, Inc., Publishers. Pp.90-92)

DIC   Dickerson, Caitlin. 2015. "National Public Radio." www.npr.org. June 22. Accessed June 15, 2020. https://www.npr.org/2015/06/22/415194765/u-s-troops-tested-by-race-in-secret-world-war-ii-chemical-experiments.

ENR   Enright, W. J. 1943. "New Year Brings In Heavier Taxes."
           The New York Times, January 3: 10.

FOR   Ford, Daniel. 2016. Tales of the Flying Tigers: Five Books
           About the American Volunteer Group, Mercenary Heroes of
           Burma and China. CreateSpace Independent Publishing
           Platform.

FRA   Francillon, Rene J. 1988. *McDonnell Douglas Aircraft Since
           1920. Vol. 1.* Annapolis: Naval Institute Press.

GLU   Glusman, John A. 2005. *Conduct Under Fire.* New York:
           Viking Penguin.

GRO   Groom, Winston. 2005. 1942 *The Year That Tried Men's
           Souls.* New York: Atlantic Monthly Press.

HAM   Hammond, William M. 1991-1995. *The Women's Army
           Corps. Brochure*, Washington D.C.: Center of Military
           History United States Army.

HOL   Holt, Jane. 1943. "The ABC of Point Rationing." *The New
           York Times,* February 21: 44.

HUL   Hulen, Bertram D. 1943. "Standley Spoke on His Own, Says
           Welles, Avoiding Stand." *The New York Times*, March 10: 1,
           5.

KHS   2001. *Kansas Historical Society.* November. Accessed
           September 16, 2019.
           https://www.kshs.org/kansapedia/prohibition/14523.

MC   Mayo Clinic. *1998-2020. Mayoclinic.org.* Accessed 04 07,
           2020. https://www.mayoclinic.org/diseases-
           conditions/pyloric-stenosis/symptoms-causes/syc-20351416.

MIL   Miller, David. 2008. Mercy Ships: The Untold Story or Prisoner-of-War Exchanges in World War II. New York: Continuum.

MUE   Mueller, Robert. 1989. Air Force Bases, Volume 1. Washington, DC: Office of Air Force History, United States Air Force.

MUR   Murray, Williamson, and Allan R. Millett. 2001. *A War to be Won: Fighting the Second World War.* Belknap Press: An Imprint of Harvard University Press.

NCN   *The New Castle News.* 1942. "Kidnap Hoax." September 18: 1.

NYT   The New York Times

(12/18/1942) *The New York Times.* 1942. "'A' Gasoline Cards May Be Suspended In Eastern States." December 18: 1.

(03/05/1942) *The New York Times.* 1942. "Cuba To Get Supplies." March 5: 4.

(06/17/1942) *The New York Times.* 1942. "Cuban Navy Saves 267." June 17: 12.

(02/09/1943) *The New York Times.* 1943. "Deduction Allowed For Medical Expense." February 9: 18.

(03/31/1972) *The New York Times.* 1972. "Gabriel Heatter, Radio Newsman, Dies." March 31: 32.

(04/23/1942) *The New York Times.* 1942. "Gasoline Rations Will Start May 15." April 23: 16.

(07/09/1943) *The New York Times.* 1943. "Haight, 17,

Youngest to Die in the Chair; 2 Other Lads, 18 and 19, Also Pay Penalty." July 9: 19.

(01/02/1942) *The New York Times*. 1942. "Rubber Shortage Expected in U.S." January 2: 47.

(01/15/1943) *The New York Times*. 1943. "Shortage Of Meat Expected To Grow." January 15: 14L.

03/01/1943) *The New York Times*. 1943. "Stores Prepared to Aid Housewives." March 1: 13.

(07/13/1942) *The New York Times*. 1942. "U.S. to Send Arms to Cuba." July 13: 3.

(01/04/1942) *The New York Times*. 1942. "War Days for the Motorist." January 4: Section 10, page 1.

(09/16/1942) *The New York Times*. 1942. "Youth Admits Kidnapping And Killing Girls, 7 and 8." September 16: 1, 19.

10/25/1983: *New York Times*. 1983. "H. Ford Wilkins, Ex-Reporter." October 25: 34.

PB   n.d. playbill.com. Accessed April 25, 2020. https://www.playbill.com/production/the-doughgirls-lyceum-theatre-vault-0000007207.

ROB   Roberts, Robert B. 1988. Encyclopedia of Historic Forts--The Military, Pioneer, and Trading Posts of the United States. New York: Macmillan Publishing Company.

ROM   Rominiecki, Amanda. 2017. "APG News." apgnews.com. January 5. Accessed June 15, 2020. apgnews.com/special-focus/apg-100/chemical-biological-history.

SAB   Sabar, Ariel. 2003. "A military base's last line of toxic defense: bluegills." *The Baltimore Sun*, January 20.

SCH   Schifferle, Peter J. 2010. America's School for War: Fort Leavenworth, Officer Education, and Victory in World War II. Lawrence: University Press of Kansas.

SMI1   Smith, Jean Edward. 2008. *FDR*. New York: Random House Trade Paperbacks.

SMI2   Smith, Susan L. 2008. "Mustard Gas and American Race-Based Human Experimentation in World War II." *The Journal of Law Medicine & Ethics* 36: 517-21.

STE   Steiner, George R. 1991. "Letter to the Key West Art and Historical Society." Minneapolis, January 9.

TMN   *The Miami News*. 1942. "Army Probes Crash Here Killing 5, Injuring 4." September 23: 11.

TUP   *The United Press*. 1943. "Envoy Warns at Moscow Of Lend-Lease Effect Here." The New York Times, March 9: 1, 5.

THO   Thomsen, Brian M., ed. 2003. Blue and Gray at Sea Naval Memoirs of the Civil War. New York: Forge.

TYL   Tyler, Orville Z. 1951. *The History of Fort Leavenworth, 1937-1951*. Fort Leavenworth: The Command and General Staff College.

WIL   Wilkins, H. Ford. 1941. "Defenders Were Ready." *The New York Times*, December 23: 2

Printed in Poland
by Amazon Fulfillment
Poland Sp. z o.o., Wrocław